8th Workshop on Patent and Scientific Literature Translation 2019

Held at Machine Translation Summit XVII

Dublin, Ireland
20 August 2019

ISBN: 978-1-5108-9250-7

Printed from e-media with permission by:

Curran Associates, Inc.
57 Morehouse Lane
Red Hook, NY 12571

Some format issues inherent in the e-media version may also appear in this print version.

Printed by Curran Associates, Inc. (2019)

For permission requests, please contact the Association for Computational Linguistics at the address below.

Association for Computational Linguistics
209 N. Eighth Street
Stroudsburg, Pennsylvania 18360

Phone: 1-570-476-8006
Fax: 1-570-476-0860

acl@aclweb.org

Additional copies of this publication are available from:

Curran Associates, Inc.
57 Morehouse Lane
Red Hook, NY 12571 USA
Phone: 845-758-0400
Fax: 845-758-2633
Email: curran@proceedings.com
Web: www.proceedings.com

Machine Translation Summit XVII

Proceedings of The 8th Workshop on
Patent and Scientific Literature Translation
http://www.aamtjapio.com/pslt2019/

20 August, 2019
Dublin, Ireland

Proceedings of The 8th Workshop on Patent and Scientific Literature Translation

http://www.aamtjapio.com/pslt2019/

20 August, 2019
Dublin, Ireland

Engaging Content
Engaging People

DCU

European Association for Machine Translation

Preface from the co-chairs of the workshop

The Workshops on Patent and Scientific Literature Translation (PSLT), beginning as Workshops on Patent Translation (WPT), had been held biennially from 2005 to 2017 as parts of Machine Translation Summits. While patent information is still one of the major application areas of machine translation, the need for translation of different kinds of scientific literature has been increasing rapidly. The workshop covers a wide range of topics related to translation of scientific literature including patents, scientific articles, and technical reports, which have common characteristics as well as their own characteristics.

This year's workshop hosted three invited talks from various aspects: utilization of machine translation for patents/scientific literatures, transferring NLP methods across languages by machine translation techniques, and multilingual NLP in biomedical domains. Each of three invited speakers (Christof Monz, University of Amsterdam, Yohei Matsutani, Japan Patent Office, and Aurélie Névéol, LIMSI-CNRS) involves, but not limited to, multiple topics described above, and thus we believe that these invited talks give us a broader view of the state-of-the-art patent and scientific literature translation. The workshop also accepted four contributed papers that deal with interesting topics in line with current trends: three are on neural machine translation by hybrid model of data parallel approach and model parallel approach, transductive data-selection algorithms, and a multi-hop attention, respectively, and one is on how patent professionals use gist machine translation for decision making. We have organized these invited talks and scientific papers into three sessions. We hope that this workshop will contribute to mutual interaction and progress of machine translation and the fields applying machine translation.

We express our sincere appreciation to the invited speakers, the authors of the contributed papers, the Program Committee Members of this workshop, and organizing members of the MT Summit 2019.

Workshop Co-chairs
Takehito Utsuro
Katsuhito Sudoh
Takashi Tsunakawa

Organizers

Program Committee Co-Chairs

Takehito Utsuro	University of Tsukuba, Japan
Katsuhito Sudoh	Nara Institute of Science and Technology, Japan
Takashi Tsunakawa	Shizuoka University, Japan

Program Committee Members

Hailong Cao	Harbin Institute of Technology, China
Key-Sun Choi	Korea Advanced Institute of Science and Technology, Republic of Korea
Chenhui Chu	Osaka University, Japan
Hiroshi Echizen'ya	Hokkai-Gakuen University, Japan
Terumasa Ehara	Ehara NLP Research Laboratory, Japan
Isao Goto	NHK (Japan Broadcasting Corporation), Japan
Eduard Hovy	Carnegie Mellon University, USA
Kenji Imamura	National Institute of Information and Communications Technology (NICT), Japan
Satoshi Kinoshita	Japan Patent Information Organization (Japio), Japan
Sadao Kurohashi	Kyoto University, Japan
Toshiaki Nakazawa	The University of Tokyo, Japan
Takashi Ninomiya	Ehime University, Japan
Bruno Pouliquen	World Intellectual Property Organization
Svetlana Sheremetyeva	South Ural State Universtiy, Russia
Jun'ichi Tsujii	National Institute of Advanced Industrial Science and Technology (AIST), Japan
Shoichi Yokoyama	Yamagata University, Japan
Jiajun Zhang	Chinese Academy of Sciences, China

Contents

Invited Talk:
Neural Machine Translation for Dynamic Domains

Christof Monz
University of Amsterdam

Profile

Christof Monz is an associate professor in computer science at the Informatics Institute, University of Amsterdam. His research interests lie in the area of multilingual natural language processing and machine translation in particular. Prior to joining the University of Amsterdam he worked as a lecturer at Queen Mary University of London and as a post-doctoral research fellow at the University of Maryland Institute for Advanced Computer Studies (UMIACS). He received a PhD in Computer Science from the University of Amsterdam in 2003.

Invited Talk:
Utilization of Machine Translation in the Japan Patent Office toward improvement of accessibility for Patent Information

Yohei Matsutani
Japan Patent Office

Profile

Yohei Matsutani has served as Deputy Director at the Patent Information Policy Planning Office, Policy Planning and Coordination Department in the Japan Patent Office since July 2018. He engages in planning policies related to the translation of patent information. He joined the JPO as a patent examiner in 2004. In his 15 years' career in the JPO, he has been involved in the patent examination of medical devices, analytical instruments.

Invited Talk:
Biomedical Natural Language processing in multiple languages: contribution of multilingual corpus and machine translation

Aurélie Névéol
LIMSI-CNRS

Profile

Aurélie Névéol is a Senior Staff Scientist at the Centre National pour la Recherche Scientifique (CNRS). She received an MSc in Linguistics in 2002 and a PhD in Computer Science in 2005. She has more than 10 years experience in biomedical Natural Language Processing Research and has addressed the analysis of biomedical text from the literature and from Electronic Health Records in French and in English. Recently, she has been focusing on clinical NLP for languages other than English. She has contributed to the development of representations of clinical information to support information extraction from EHR text, which can then be used for high throughput phenotyping. In the course of her work she has also contributed to the evaluation of research methods and workflows through her participation in the H2020 MIROR project and international evaluation campaigns such as CLEF eHealth and the biomedical task at WMT.

Hybrid Data-Model Parallel Training for Sequence-to-Sequence Recurrent Neural Network Machine Translation

Junya Ono **Masao Utiyama** **Eiichiro Sumita**

National Institute of Information and Communications Technology
3-5 Hikaridai, Seika-cho, Soraku-gun, Kyoto 619-0289, Japan
{junya.ono, mutiyama, eiichiro.sumita}@nict.go.jp

Abstract

Reduction of training time is an important issue in many tasks like patent translation involving neural networks. Data parallelism and model parallelism are two common approaches for reducing training time using multiple graphics processing units (GPUs) on one machine. In this paper, we propose a hybrid data-model parallel approach for sequence-to-sequence (Seq2Seq) recurrent neural network (RNN) machine translation. We apply a model parallel approach to the RNN encoder-decoder part of the Seq2Seq model and a data parallel approach to the attention-softmax part of the model. We achieved a speed-up of 4.13 to 4.20 times when using 4 GPUs compared with the training speed when using 1 GPU without affecting machine translation accuracy as measured in terms of BLEU scores.

1 Introduction

Neural machine translation (NMT) has been widely used owing to its high accuracy. A downside of NMT is it requires a long training time. For instance, training a Seq2Seq RNN machine translation (MT) with attention (Luong et al., 2015) could take over 10 days using 10 million sentence pairs.

A natural solution to this is to use multiple GPUs. There are currently two common approaches for reducing the training time of NMT models. One approach is by using data parallel approach, while the other approach is through the use of the model parallel approach.

The data parallel approach is common in many neural network (NN) frameworks. For instance, OpenNMT-lua (Klein et al., 2017)[1], an NMT toolkit, uses multiple GPUs in training NN models using the data parallel approach. In this approach, the same model is distributed to different GPUs as replicas, and each replica is updated using different data. Afterward, the gradients obtained from each replica are accumulated, and parameters are updated.

The model parallel approach has been used for training a Seq2Seq RNN MT with attention (Wu et al., 2016). In this approach, the model is distributed across multiple GPUs, that is, each GPU has only a part of the model. Subsequently, the same data are processed by all GPUs so that each GPU estimates the parameters it is responsible for.

In this paper, we propose a hybrid data-model parallel approach for Seq2Seq RNN MT with attention. We apply a model parallel approach to the RNN encoder-decoder part of the Seq2Seq model and a data parallel approach to the attention-softmax part of the model.

The structure of this paper is as follows: In Section 2, we describe related work. In Section 3, first, we discuss the baseline model with/without data/model parallelism. Afterward, we present the proposed hybrid data-model parallel approach. In Section 4, we present a comparison of these parallel approaches and demonstrate the scalability of the proposed hybrid parallel approach. Section 5 presents the conclusion of the work.

2 Related Work

The accuracy of NN models improves as the model sizes and data increases. Thus, it is

[1] https://github.com/OpenNMT/OpenNMT

necessary to use multiple GPUs when training NN models within a short turnaround time.

There are two common approaches for using multiple GPUs in training. One is data parallelism, involving sending different data to different GPUs with the replicas of the same model. The other is model parallelism, involving sending the same data to different GPUs having different parts of the model.

2.1 Data parallelism

In this approach, each GPU has a replica of the same NN model. The gradients obtained from each model on each GPU are accumulated after a backward process, and the parameters are synchronized and updated.

The advantage of using this model is that it can be applied to any NN model because it does not depend on the model structure. In particular, it can be applied to many models such as Seq2Seq RNN and Inception Network (Abadi et al., 2016). Many deep neural network (DNN) frameworks implement data parallelism.

While data parallelism is general and powerful, it is subject to synchronization issues among multiple GPUs as the model size or the number of model parameters increases. Note that when using multiple machines, asynchronous updates may be used in reducing synchronization costs. However, we focus on using multiple GPUs on one machine, where synchronous updates are generally better than asynchronous updates.

To reduce the synchronization costs relative to all training costs, it is necessary to train models using a large mini-batch size. However, the mini-batch size is bounded by the GPU memory. Furthermore, large mini-batch sizes in general, make convergence difficult and can worsen accuracy of the tasks (Krizhevsky, 2014; Keskar et al., 2017).

Another important factor to be considered is the ratio of processing time needed for synchronization and forward-backward process on each GPU. If synchronization takes much longer than the forward-backward process, the advantage of using multiple GPUs diminishes.

In summary, depending on models, data parallelism may not work effectively. In such a case, there are methods that can be used to achieve synchronization after several mini-batches or to overlap backward and synchronization process at the same time (Ott et al., 2018). However, these advanced synchronization methods are out of the scope of this study.

2.2 Model parallelism

In this approach, each GPU has different parameters (and computation) of different parts of a model. Most of the communication occurs when passing intermediate results between GPUs. In other words, multiple GPUs do not need to synchronize the values of the parameters.

In contrast to data parallelism, most DNN frameworks do not implement automatic model parallelism. Programmers have to implement it depending on the model and available GPUs.

Model parallelism needs special care when assigning different layers to different GPUs. For example, each long short-term memory (LSTM) layer may be placed on each GPU in case of stacked-LSTMs in encoder-decoder NN. Wu et al. (2016) have already proposed similar model parallelism for Seq2Seq RNN MT, although they did not describe the actual speed-up achieved.

The scalability of model parallelism is better than that of data parallelism when it works effectively. In data parallelism, when we increase the number of samples in each mini-batch to N times, we expect less than N times speed-up due to synchronization costs.

In contrast, we can expect more than N times speed-up when using model parallelism, owing to the following two reasons. First, we can increase the mini-batch size as in the case of data parallelism. Second, each GPU is able to compute different layers of the model without requiring synchronization.

2.3 Automatic hybrid parallelism, distributed training, and Transformer

While we focus on hybrid data-model parallelism for Seq2Seq RNN MT in this paper, Wang et al. (2018) have proposed an approach for automatically conducting hybrid data-model parallelism. Applying their method to Seq2Seq RNN MT would be the focus of our future work.

While we focus on parallelism on one machine in this paper, using multiple machines is also a good way of achieving a short turnaround time in training. Ott et al. (2018) reported that a significant speed-up can be obtained while maintaining translation accuracy using data parallelism on 16 machines.

While the Transformer model has recently been demonstrated to have a superior translation performance to the Seq2Seq RNN MT with attention (Vaswani et al., 2017), we focus on how to combine data parallelism and model parallelism in Seq2Seq RNN MT with attention. We believe the proposed hybrid parallel approach to be applicable to the Transformer translation model because Transformer also has an encoder, decoder, and softmax layers. However, we would leave the application of the proposed hybrid data-model parallel approach to Transformer as a part of our future work.

3 Model Structure and Parallelism

3.1 Baseline model

Attention-based NMT has improved translation accuracy compared with the sequence-to-sequence NMT without attention model (Bahdanau et al., 2015; Luong et al., 2015).

Figure 1 shows our baseline model (Luong et al., 2015). The decoder side of this model uses the input-feeding approach, where the hidden state of attention is concatenated with the target word embedding before being input into the first LSTM layer.

Data parallelism can be applied to this baseline model easily. We place each replica of this model on each GPU. Next, the input parallel texts are distributed equally to different GPUs. Finally, synchronization of parameter values is conducted after each forward-backward process.

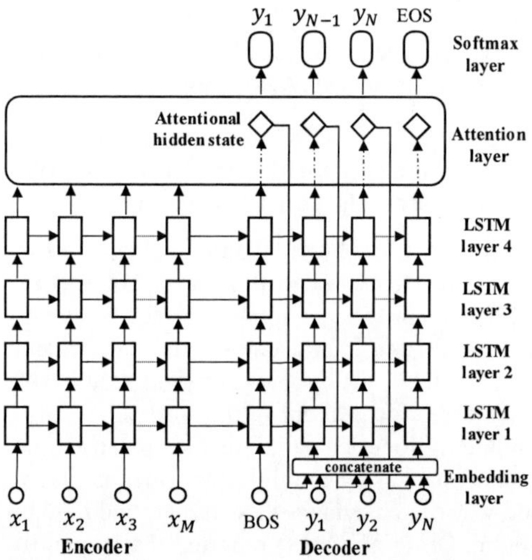

Figure 1. Our baseline model, the attention-based encoder-decoder model (Luong et al., 2015). This model consists of stacked-LSTMs containing 4 layers with the input-feeding approach. The hidden state of attention is concatenated with the target word embedding before being input into the first LSTM layer

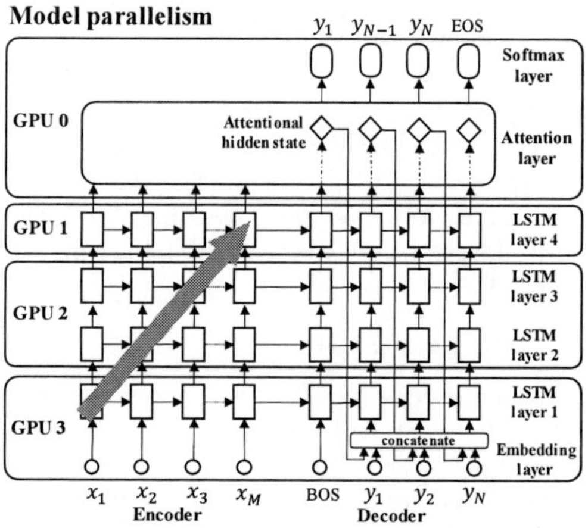

Figure 2. Model parallelism on 4 GPUs for the baseline model of Figure 1. The same depth layer in the encoder-decoder part is placed on the same GPU. The encoder side allows efficient parallelism, while the decoder part does not due to input-feeding.

Figure 2 shows an application of model parallelism to the baseline model on 4 GPUs. In the figure, we assign different layers in the encoder-decoder part to different 3 GPUs. We also assign the attention and softmax layers to 1 GPU. This assignment is based on the fact that the attention-softmax part requires a relatively large GPU memory.

The model parallel approach is effective in this case because there are many parameters in the attention-based encoder-decoder model. Let U be a certain value representing the number of parameters, the embedding layer has 2U parameters, each LSTM layer has 8U parameters (a total of 32U parameters), and the attention-softmax part has 4U parameters. When using model parallelism, it is not necessary to synchronize these parameters. We only have to pass intermediate results between different GPUs.

Note that the green arrow in Figure 2 is pointing to the upper right direction. It indicates that the computation of one node can start immediately after the left and down nodes finish their computation. In this way, in the encoder side, GPUs can work without waiting for the completion of the computation in the previous steps.

In contrast, the nodes in the decoder side cannot start performing their assigned computations until all nodes related to the previous target words finish their computation. This is due to the input-feeding approach employed. For instance, the target word embedding of y_2 needs to be concatenated with the attentional hidden state of y_1 before being input into the first LSTM layer.

3.2 Proposed model for hybrid parallelism

Herein, we propose our hybrid parallelism for Seq2Seq RNN MT. First, we remove input-feeding in the decoder side of the baseline model, and then we introduce our hybrid parallelism.
Figure 3 shows our model for hybrid parallelism. First, we employ model parallelism in calculating the states of hidden nodes for all steps in both encoder and decoder sides. Afterward, we apply data parallelism in calculating attention scores, context vectors, and softmax for getting target words. Note that this is possible because all target words are given beforehand in the training phase.

As stated earlier, we remove input-feeding in the decoder of the baseline model (Luong et al., 2015). While input-feeding has been proposed by Luong et al. (2015) and has shown its advantages in translation accuracy, it has been found to be unsuitable for parallelism. Removing input-feeding removes the dependency of calculation on previous steps in the decoder side. The green arrows going to the upper-right direction show that the computation of a node can start immediately after completion of left and down nodes computation in both encoder and decoder sides. By comparing Figures 2 with 3, we observe that removing input-feeding allows model parallelism to perform better parallel computation. Note that the proposed NMT model has already been proposed by Luong et al. (2015) as a simpler model than the baseline model with input-feeding. However, in the section on the experimentation, we show that removing input-feeding does not affect translation accuracy in terms of BLEU scores obtained.

We now present how we alternate model parallelism and data parallelism on the same 4 GPUs. This is the most important point in the proposed hybrid parallelism implementation.

First, we use 4 GPUs for model parallelism. The source and target word embedding layers and 4 LSTM layers are placed on 3 GPUs as shown in Figure 3. The remaining GPU (GPU 3 in Figure 3) stores the hidden states of all steps in the encoder-decoder part.

After the forward process of all hidden states, we move to data parallelism. The intermediate results of all hidden states for all data in the mini-batch are distributed equally to 4 GPUs. While all GPUs have replicas of the same network structure,

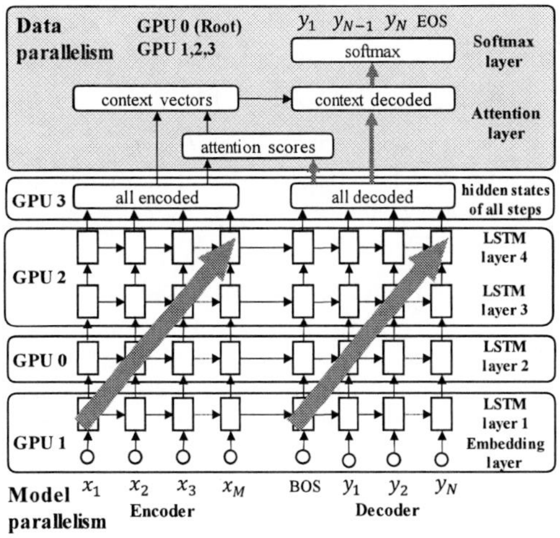

Figure 3. Proposed model for hybrid parallelism.

as shown in Figure 3, we use GPU 0 as the root for accumulating and synchronizing all parameter values relating to the calculation of attention scores, context vectors, softmax, and so on. The alternation of data parallelism and model parallelism on the backward process goes in a similar but opposite direction.

As mentioned in Section 3.1, the encoder-decoder part has much more parameters than the attention-softmax part. This is the reason why we use model parallelism on the encoder-decoder part and data parallelism on the attention-softmax part.

We now describe closely how we obtain the attention scores and so on in Figure 3. We omit an explanation of model parallelism for stacked-LSTM layers because it is straightforward.

Let $\boldsymbol{\alpha}$ be "attention scores" in Figure 3, it is a concatenation of all attention coefficients of all decoder steps. We employ the attention coefficient defined as global attention (Luong et al., 2015).

$$\boldsymbol{\alpha} = (\alpha_{1,\dots,}\alpha_{i,\dots,}\alpha_N) = \text{Softmax}(\widehat{\boldsymbol{\alpha}}) \quad (1)$$

$$\widehat{\boldsymbol{\alpha}} = \boldsymbol{H}^T\, W_\alpha\, \boldsymbol{S} \quad (2)$$

where $\boldsymbol{S} = (S_{1,\dots,}S_{j,\dots,}S_M)$ denotes the concatenation of all hidden states of length M in the encoder side, $\boldsymbol{H} = (H_{1,\dots,}H_{i,\dots,}H_N)$ denotes the concatenation of all hidden states of length N in the decoder side, and W_α denotes a parameter matrix. Note that we can calculate $\boldsymbol{\alpha}$ at once after obtaining the hidden states of all steps in the encoder-decoder part in the forward process.

The "context vectors" $\boldsymbol{C}$ in Figure 3 can be defined as

$$\boldsymbol{C} = (C_{1,\dots,}C_{i,\dots,}C_N) = \boldsymbol{\alpha} \cdot \boldsymbol{S} \quad (3)$$

The "context decoded" $\boldsymbol{H_c}$ in Figure 3 can be defined as

$$\boldsymbol{H_c} = (H_{c1,\cdots,}H_{ci,\cdots,}H_{cN}) \\ = \tanh(W_c[\boldsymbol{H}; \boldsymbol{C}]) \tag{4}$$

where W_c denotes a parameter matrix. Finally, the conditional probabilities $\boldsymbol{P}$ of the target sentence words can be computed as

$$\boldsymbol{P} = (P_{1,\cdots,}P_{i,\cdots,}P_N) = \text{Softmax}\{F_c(\boldsymbol{H_c})\} \tag{5}$$

$$P_i = P(y_i|y_{1,\cdots,}y_{i-1,}\,\boldsymbol{x}) \tag{6}$$

where F_c denotes a liner function; $\boldsymbol{x}$ denotes the source sentence in the encoder side; $\mathbf{y} = (y_{1,\cdots,}y_N)$ represents the target sentence in the decoder side.

4 Experiments

We evaluate training speed, convergence speed, and translation accuracy to compare the performance of the proposed approach as shown in Figure 3 (hereafter referred to as HybridNMT) with the baseline model shown in Figure 1 with/without data/model parallelism. We also augment the proposed approach in Figure 3 with input-feeding (hereafter referred to as HybridNMTIF). HybridNMTIF lacks the parallelism in the decoder side but has input-feeding. Consequently, comparing HybridNMT with HybridNMTIF clarifies the advantages of the proposed hybrid parallelism.

4.1 Data statistics

We used datasets of WMT14 (Bojar et al., 2014)[2] and WMT17 (Bojar et al., 2017)[3] English-German shared news translation tasks in the experiments. Both datasets were pre-processed using the scripts of the Marian toolkit (Junczys-Dowmunt et al., 2018)[4]. Table 1 shows the number of sentences in these datasets. For the WMT17 dataset, first, we duplicated the provided parallel corpus, and then we augmented the parallel corpus with the pseudo-parallel corpus obtained using back-translation (Sennrich et al., 2016a) of the provided German monolingual data of 10 million (M) sentences. Overall, we used 19 M sentence pairs in the training. We also used the word vocabulary of 32 thousand (K) types from joint source and target byte pair encoding (BPE; Sennrich et al., 2016b).

Dataset en-de	Sentences	
	WMT14	WMT17
Training (original)	4492K	4561K
Training (monolingual)	—	10000K
Training (all)	4492K	19122K
Development	3000	2999
Test	3003	3004

Table 1. Datasets of WMT14 and WMT17.

Parameter	Value
word embedding size	512
RNN cell type	Stacked-LSTMs
hidden state size	1024
encoder/decoder depth	4
attention type	global
optimizer	Adam
initial learing rate	0.001
learing rate decay	0.7

Table 2. Model parameters.

4.2 Parameter settings

Both the baseline model and HybridNMT are trained with the same hyperparameters, as shown in Table 2. To prevent over-fitting, we set a dropout of 0.3 (Srivastava et al., 2014) and used Adam (Kingma and Ba, 2015) of the following setting: $\beta_1 = 0.9$, $\beta_2 = 0.999$, and $\epsilon = $ 1e-8.

All models were subject to the same decay schedule of learning rate because the convergence speed generally depends on it. In this experiment, the learning rate was multiplied by a fixed value of 0.7 when the perplexity of the development data increased in a fixed interval; an interval of 5,000 and 20,000 batches for WMT14 and WMT17, respectively, reflecting the difference in the number of sentences in these training data.

The machine type used for training had 4 GPUs of NVIDIA Tesla V100 and was capable of performing direct data transfer among all GPUs using NVLink. We implemented the baseline model with/without data/model parallelism, HybridNMT, and HybridNMTIF in MXNet v1.3.0 (Chen et al., 2015)[5]. We also used OpenNMT-lua v0.9.2 (Klein et al., 2017) for comparing the models because it implements the baseline model with/without data parallelism. We used the default synchronous mode in OpenNMT-lua and the SGD optimizer as the default settings of the OpenNMT-lua.

[2] http://www.statmt.org/wmt14/translation-task.html
[3] http://www.statmt.org/wmt17/translation-task.html
[4] https://github.com/marian-nmt/marian-examples/tree/master/wmt2017-uedin
[5] https://github.com/apache/incubator-mxnet

4.3 Comparison of training speed

Table 3 summarizes the main results of our experiment. In Table 3, "SRC tokens / sec" indicates the number of source tokens processed in one second. This is a standard measure for evaluating training speed; it is also implemented in OpenNMT-lua. "Scaling factor" stands for the ratio of "SRC tokens / sec" against that of one GPU. The mini-batch sizes were determined by the available GPU memories. Note that mini-batch sizes were about 4 times when using 4 GPUs compared with those obtained when using 1 GPU.

First, the scaling factors of HybridNMT were higher than those of data/model parallelism. They were 4.13 and 4.20 for WMT14 and WMT17 datasets, respectively. This indicates that our hybrid parallel method for Seq2Seq RNN MT is faster than only data/model parallel approaches. Note also that these scaling factors were higher than the number of GPUs (4). This demonstrates the effectiveness of the proposed hybrid parallelism.

Second, the processing speed and scaling factors of OpenNMT-lua and those obtained from our implementation were similar. Table 4 shows that BLEU scores are comparable. These indicate that our implementation is appropriate.

Third, the scaling factors of model parallelism were better than those of data parallelism were. For WMT14, the scaling factor of data parallelism in our implementation was 1.60 and that of model parallelism was 2.32. This indicates that model parallelism is faster than data parallelism for Seq2Seq RNN MT. We attribute this to the synchronization costs of a large number of parameters. The number of parameters used in the baseline model was 142 M and that for HybridNMT was 138 M.

Finally, the scaling factors of HybridNMTIF were between those of HybridNMT and the baseline model with model parallelism. This indicates that the proposed hybrid data-model parallel approach is faster than speed obtained when using only model parallelism, even when the same network structure is used. Furthermore, removing input-feeding allows for faster training speed.

4.4 Comparison of convergence speed

Figure 4 shows the convergence speed for different methods applied to WMT14 and WMT17. The horizontal axis represents wall-clock training time in hours. The vertical axis represents the perplexity of development data. We measured the perplexities at the ends of epochs, represented as points in the graphs.

HybridNMT converges faster compared with other methods. This, in addition to Table 3, implies that HybridNMT is better than other methods in terms of training and convergence speed. Other findings: data parallelism as implemented in both OpenNMT-lua and our implementation performed poorly as shown in Figure 4 as well as in Table 3. The perplexities obtained with model parallelism became similar to those of our hybrid parallelism after long runs. Finally, the convergence speed of HybridNMTIF was between those of HybridNMT and the baseline model with model parallelism. This indicates that the proposed hybrid data-model parallel approach is faster than model parallelism, and removing input-feeding leads to faster convergence.

	SRC tokens / sec		Scaling factor		Mini-batch size	
	WMT14	WMT17	WMT14	WMT17	WMT14	WMT17
OpenNMT-lua						
baseline (1GPU)	2979	2757	—	—	64	64
w/ data parallelism	4881	4715	1.64	1.71	256	256
Our implementation						
baseline (1GPU)	2826	2550	—	—	64	64
w/ data parallelism	4515	4330	1.60	1.70	256	256
w/ model parallelism	6570	6397	2.32	2.51	224	224
HybridNMTIF	9688	9109	3.43	3.57	224	224
HybridNMT	**11672**	**10716**	**4.13**	**4.20**	224	224

Table 3. Results of training speed and scaling factors.

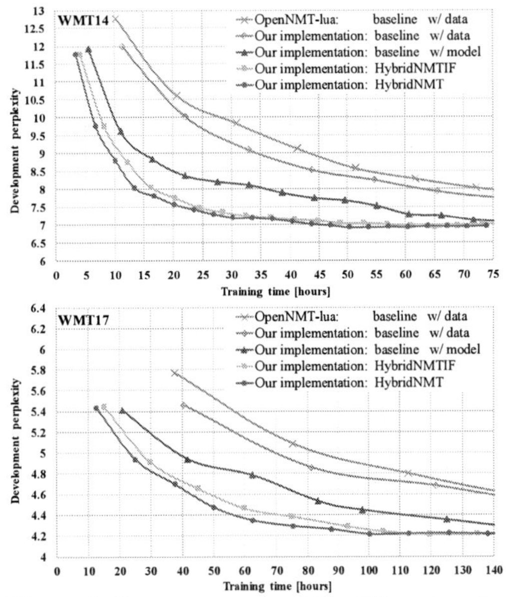

Figure 4. Convergence speed for different methods.

OpenNMT-lua BLEU scores		WMT 14 development (test2013) b = 3	b = 6	b = 9	b = 12	b = 15	b = 18	WMT 17 development (test2016) b = 3	b = 6	b = 9	b = 12	b = 15	b = 18
(length, coverage) normalization	(1.0, 0.0)	21.80	**21.83**	21.81	21.74	21.65	21.54	31.70	**31.86**	31.73	31.73	31.65	31.55
	(0.8, 0.0)	21.80	21.80	21.77	21.71	21.60	21.47	31.70	31.85	31.73	31.71	31.62	31.53
	(0.6, 0.0)	21.77	21.77	21.69	21.63	21.50	21.37	31.68	31.81	31.72	31.68	31.57	31.48
	(0.4, 0.0)	21.77	21.75	21.66	21.58	21.44	21.31	31.68	31.79	31.67	31.61	31.49	31.40
	(0.2, 0.0)	21.77	21.75	21.65	21.56	21.42	21.28	31.65	31.79	31.64	31.59	31.48	31.38
	(0.0, 0.0)	21.75	21.73	21.65	21.54	21.40	21.27	31.63	31.75	31.60	31.57	31.44	31.36
	(0.2, 0.2)	21.14	21.08	21.18	21.12	21.10	21.15	30.87	30.94	30.84	30.85	30.79	30.70

HybridNMT BLEU scores		WMT 14 development (test2013) b = 3	b = 6	b = 9	b = 12	b = 15	b = 18	WMT 17 development (test2016) b = 3	b = 6	b = 9	b = 12	b = 15	b = 18
length normalization	1.0	22.43	22.75	22.72	22.75	**22.79**	22.75	32.23	32.60	32.61	**32.73**	32.65	32.60
	0.8	22.43	22.71	22.63	22.67	22.67	22.63	32.20	32.52	32.59	32.70	32.67	32.62
	0.6	22.35	22.62	22.56	22.55	22.54	22.50	32.16	32.44	32.51	32.56	32.55	32.49
	0.4	22.29	22.50	22.43	22.38	22.40	22.35	32.10	32.32	32.36	32.38	32.38	32.32
	0.2	22.26	22.37	22.29	22.24	22.26	22.20	32.02	32.19	32.25	32.26	32.21	32.16
	0.0	22.23	22.27	22.14	22.11	22.13	22.04	32.01	32.11	32.18	32.16	32.09	31.98

Table 4. BLEU scores obtained using different hyperparameters for WMT14 and WMT17 development data. The upper half shows the results obtained by OpenNMT-lua whereas the lower half is for the proposed HybridNMT. "b" stands for the beam size.

4.5 Translation accuracy

As mentioned in Section 3, the proposed Hybrid NMT uses a simpler model structure than that of the baseline model. We have shown in Figure 4 that the perplexities of HybridNMT are comparable and even lower than those of the baseline model with data/model parallelism in a limited training time owing to its faster convergence speed. Herein, we compare the translation accuracy as measured by BLEU scores.

To compare BLEU scores, first, we selected the models for the proposed HybridNMT and OpenNMT-lua based on the information provided in Figure 4. In other words, we selected the models with the lowest development perplexities.

Table 4 shows BLEU scores on the development data obtained by OpenNMT-lua and HybridNMT with diverse hyperparameters. The beam size was changed from 3 to 18. OpenNMT-lua used the same normalization method of GNMT (Wu et al., 2016). Its optimal parameters for the development data were as follows: the beam sizes were 6 and 12 for WMT14 and WMT17, respectively; the length normalization values were both 1.0; and the coverage normalization values were both 0. The proposed HybridNMT used the same normalization of Marian (Junczys-Dowmunt et al., 2018), which simply divided the model score using a length normalization factor. Its optimal parameters were as follows: the beam sizes were 15 and 12 for WMT14 and WMT17, respectively and the length penalties were 1.0 for both datasets, implying that the model score was divided by the number of target words to get the normalized score.

System	Reference	WMT14 test2014	WMT17 test2017
RNNsearch-LV	Jean et al. (2015)	19.4	—
Deep-Att	Zhou et al. (2016)	20.6	—
Luong	Luong et al. (2015)	20.9	—
BPE-Char	Chung et al. (2016)	21.5	—
seq2seq	Britz et al. (2017)	22.19	—
OpenNMT-lua	Klein et al. (2017)	19.34	—
	Our experiment	21.85	25.92
HybridNMT	**Our experiment**	**22.71**	**26.91**
GNMT	Wu et al. (2016)	24.61	—
Nematus (deep model)	Sennrich et al. (2017)	—	26.6
Marian (deep model)	Junczys et al. (2018)	—	27.7

Table 5. BLEU scores published regarding Seq2Seq RNN MT.

We measured BLEU scores for WMT14 and WMT17 test data using the parameters stated above. Table 5 shows the BLEU scores together with other published results on the same test data using Seq2Seq RNN MT for reference. For the WMT14 dataset, the proposed HybridNMT outperformed all the others but GNMT (Wu et al., 2016). Note that GNMT used 8 layers for the encoder-decoder part, while the proposed HybridNMT used 4 layers. Note also that the

BLEU score of OpenNMT-lua in this experiment was higher than that of Klein et al. (2017). This is probably because Klein et al. (2017) used 2 layers but we used 4 layers in our experiments. For the WMT17 dataset, the proposed HybridNMT performed comparably with other results. The results show that the translation of the proposed HybridNMT is accurate comparably with other Seq2Seq RNN MT models.

5 Conclusions

We have proposed a hybrid data-model parallel approach for Seq2Seq RNN MT. We applied model parallelism to the encoder-decoder part and data parallelism to the attention-softmax part. The experimental results show that the proposed hybrid parallel approach achieved more than 4 times speed-up in training time using 4 GPUs. This is a very good result compared with data parallelism and model parallelism whose speed-up was around 1.6-1.7 and 2.3-2.5 times when the same 4 GPUs were used. We believe the proposed hybrid approach can also be applied to the Transformer translation model because it also has the encoder, decoder, and softmax layers.

Acknowledgments

We would like to thank Atsushi Fujita and anonymous reviewers for their useful suggestions and comments in this paper.

References

Martín Abadi, Paul Barham, Jianmin Chen, Zhifeng Chen, Andy Davis, Jeffrey Dean, Matthieu Devin, Sanjay Ghemawat, Geoffrey Irving, Michael Isard, Manjunath Kudlur, Josh Levenberg, Rajat Monga, Sherry Moore, Derek G. Murray, Benoit Steiner, Paul Tucker, Vijay Vasudevan, Pete Warden, Martin Wicke, Yuan Yu, and Xiaoqiang Zheng. 2016. TensorFlow: A system for large-scale machine learning. In *Proceedings of the 12th USENIX Symposium on Operating Systems Design and Implementation (OSDI 16)*.

Dzmitry Bahdanau, Kyunghyun Cho, and Yoshua Bengio. 2015. Neural machine translation by jointly learning to align and translate. In *Proceedings of the International Conference on Learning Representations (ICLR)*.

Ondřej Bojar, Christian Buck, Christian Federmann, Barry Haddow, Philipp Koehn, Johannes Leveling, Christof Monz, Pavel Pecina, Matt Post, Herve Saint-Amand, Radu Soricut, Lucia Specia, and Aleš Tamchyna. 2014. Findings of the 2014 Workshop on Statistical Machine Translation. In *Proceedings of the Ninth Workshop on Statistical Machine Translation (WMT)*.

Ondřej Bojar, Rajen Chatterjee, Christian Federmann, Yvette Graham, Barry Haddow, Shujian Huang, Matthias Huck, Philipp Koehn, Qun Liu, Varvara Logacheva, Christof Monz, Matteo Negri, Matt Post, Raphael Rubino, Lucia Specia, and Marco Turchi. 2017. Findings of the 2017 conference on machine translation (WMT17). In *Proceedings of the Second Conference on Machine Translation (WMT), Volume 2: Shared Task Papers*.

Denny Britz, Anna Goldie, Minh-Thang Luong, and Quoc Le. 2017. Massive exploration of neural machine translation architectures. In *Proceedings of the 2017 Conference on Empirical Methods in Natural Language Processing (EMNLP)*.

Tianqi Chen, Mu Li, Yutian Li, Min Lin, Naiyan Wang, Minjie Wang, Tianjun Xiao, Bing Xu, Chiyuan Zhang, and Zheng Zhang. 2015. MXNet: A Flexible and Efficient Machine Learning Library for Heterogeneous Distributed Systems. In *arXiv:1512.01274*.

Junyoung Chung, Kyunghyun Cho, and Yoshua Bengio. 2016. A Character-Level Decoder without Explicit Segmentation for Neural Machine Translation. In *arXiv:1603.06147*.

Sébastien Jean, Kyunghyun Cho, Roland Memisevic, and Yoshua Bengio. 2015. On Using Very Large Target Vocabulary for Neural Machine Translation. In *Proceedings of the 53rd Annual Meeting of the Association for Computational Linguistics (ACL)*.

Marcin Junczys-Dowmunt, Roman Grundkiewicz, Tomasz Dwojak, Hieu Hoang, Kenneth Heafield, Tom Neckermann, Frank Seide, Ulrich Germann, Alham Fikri Aji, Nikolay Bogoychev, André F. T. Martins, and Alexandra Birch. 2018. Marian: Fast Neural Machine Translation in C++. In *arXiv:1804.00344*.

Nitish Shirish Keskar, Dheevatsa Mudigere, Jorge Nocedal, Mikhail Smelyanskiy, and Ping Tak Peter Tang. 2017. On Large-Batch Training for Deep Learning: Generalization Gap and Sharp Minima. In *arXiv:1609.04836*.

Diederik P. Kingma and Jimmy Ba. 2015. Adam: A Method for Stochastic Optimization. In *Proceedings of the International Conference on Learning Representations (ICLR).*

Guillaume Klein, Yoon Kim, Yuntian Deng, Jean Senellart, and Alexander M. Rush. 2017. OpenNMT: Open-Source Toolkit for Neural Machine Translation. In *Proceedings of the 55th Association for Computational Linguistics (ACL), System Demonstrations.*

Alex Krizhevsky. 2014. One weird trick for parallelizing convolutional neural networks. In *arXiv:1404.5997.*

Minh-Thang Luong, Hieu Pham, and Christopher D. Manning. 2015. Effective Approaches to Attention-based Neural Machine Translation. In *Proceedings of the 2015 Conference on Empirical Methods in Natural Language Processing (EMNLP).*

Myle Ott, Sergey Edunov, David Grangier, and Michael Auli. 2018. Scaling Neural Machine Translation. In *Proceedings of the Third Conference on Machine Translation (WMT): Research Papers.*

Rico Sennrich, Barry Haddow, and Alexandra Birch. 2016a. Improving Neural Machine Translation Models with Monolingual Data. In *Proceedings of the 54th Annual Meeting of the Association for Computational Linguistics (ACL).*

Rico Sennrich, Barry Haddow, and Alexandra Birch. 2016b. Neural Machine Translation of Rare Words with Subword Units. In *Proceedings of the 54th Annual Meeting of the Association for Computational Linguistics (ACL).*

Rico Sennrich, Alexandra Birch, Anna Currey, Ulrich Germann, Barry Haddow, Kenneth Heafield, Antonio Valerio Miceli Barone, and PhilipWilliams. 2017. The University of Edinburgh's Neural MT Systems for WMT17. In *Proceedings of the Second Conference on Machine Translation (WMT), Volume 2: Shared Task Papers.*

Nitish Srivastava, Geoffrey Hinton, Alex Krizhevsky, Ilya Sutskever, and Ruslan Salakhutdinov. 2014. Dropout: A Simple Way to Prevent Neural Networks from Overfitting. *Journal of Machine Learning Research, 15.*

Ashish Vaswani, Noam Shazeer, Niki Parmar, Jakob Uszkoreit, Llion Jones, Aidan N. Gomez, Łukasz Kaiser, and Illia Polosukhin. 2017. Attention Is All You Need. In *Advances in Neural Information Processing Systems (NIPS).*

Minjie Wang, Chien-chin Huang, and Jinyang Li. 2018. Unifying Data, Model and Hybrid Parallelism in Deep Learning via Tensor Tiling. In *arXiv:1805.04170.*

Yonghui Wu, Mike Schuster, Zhifeng Chen, Quoc V. Le, Mohammad Norouzi, Wolfgang Macherey, Maxim Krikun, Yuan Cao, Qin Gao, Klaus Macherey, Jeff Klingner, Apurva Shah, Melvin Johnson, Xiaobing Liu, Łukasz Kaiser, Stephan Gouws, Yoshikiyo Kato, Taku Kudo, Hideto Kazawa, Keith Stevens, George Kurian, Nishant Patil, Wei Wang, Cliff Young, Jason Smith, Jason Riesa, Alex Rudnick, Oriol Vinyals, Greg Corrado, Macduff Hughes, and Jeffrey Dean. 2016. Google's Neural Machine Translation System: Bridging the Gap between Human and Machine Translation. In *arXiv:1609.08144.*

Jie Zhou, Ying Cao, Xuguang Wang, Peng Li, and Wei Xu. 2016. Deep Recurrent Models with Fast-Forward Connections for Neural Machine Translation. In *Transactions of the Association for Computational Linguistics (TACL), 4.*

Transductive Data-Selection Algorithms for Fine-Tuning Neural Machine Translation

Alberto Poncelas and **Gideon Maillette de Buy Wenniger** and **Andy Way**
ADAPT Centre, School of Computing,
Dublin City University, Dublin, Ireland
{firstname.lastname}@adaptcentre.ie

Abstract

Machine Translation models are trained to translate a variety of documents from one language into another. However, models specifically trained for a particular characteristics of the documents tend to perform better. Fine-tuning is a technique for adapting an NMT model to some domain. In this work, we want to use this technique to adapt the model to a given test set. In particular, we are using transductive data selection algorithms which take advantage the information of the test set to retrieve sentences from a larger parallel set.

In cases where the model is available at translation time (when the test set is provided), it can be adapted with a small subset of data, thereby achieving better performance than a generic model or a domain-adapted model.

1 Introduction

Machine Translation (MT) models aim to generate a text in the target language which corresponds to the translation of a text in the source language, the test set. These models are trained with a set of parallel sentences so they can learn how to generalize and infer a translation when a new document is seen.

In the field of MT, Neural Machine Translation (NMT) models tend to achieve the best performances when large amounts of parallel sentences are used. However, relevant data is more useful than having more data. Previous studies (Silva et al., 2018) showed that models trained with in-domain sentences perform better than general-domain models.

However, training models for domains that are distant from general domains, such as scientific documents, is not always a simple task as parallel sentences are not always available. In addition, identifying the domain adds complexity if the domain of the document to be translated is too specific. The alternative explored in this work is to build models adapted to a given test set.

In order to build task-specific models, data selection algorithms play an important role as they retrieve sentences from the training data. Data selection methods can be classified (Eetemadi et al., 2015) according to the criteria considered to select sentences (e.g. select sentences of a particular domain, good quality sentences, etc.). In this work, we use the transductive (Vapnik, 1998) data selection methods which use the document to be translated to select sentences that are the most relevant for translating such text.

In some cases, the organizations in charge of translating a document are also the owner of the translation model and training data. Therefore, knowing the test set is an advantage that can be helpful for adapting the generic MT model towards the test set (Utiyama et al., 2009; Liu et al., 2012).

The approaches presented here consist of building a single NMT model and delay part of the process of training data for adapting the model when the test set is available. Although this implies increasing the time involved in translating a document, it also has some benefits.

First, using a single model causes storing multiple task-adapted models not to be necessary. Moreover, identifying the domain of the document (and so, the most appropriate model) before the translation is also avoided. In addition, due to the fine-grained adaptation, other characteristics that may have not been foreseen (e.g. formal or informal register, technical or literal vocabulary, the gender of the speaker etc.) are also considered.

This paper presents the performance of three transductive data selection algorithms (TA), applied to NMT models, showing how these models can be improved by adapting them with a small set of data. The TAs are executed using the test set as seed, but there are other approaches such as using an approximated target-side (Poncelas et al., 2018a; Poncelas et al., 2018c).

The remainder of this paper is structured as follows. In Section 2, we state the research questions that we want to investigate. Section 3 contains some insights of other works that are related to this and Section 4 describes the data selection methods used in the experiments. In Section 5 we perform an analysis of fine-tuning and in Section 6 we build the models used as baselines in later experiments. The results of the main experiments are explained in Section 7 and finally, in Section 8, we conclude and indicate further research that can be carried out in the future.

2 Research Questions

In this work, we are using a general-domain data set to build an NMT model. Then, this model will be adapted, performing fine-tuning, to two different test sets in two domains: news and health. The data used to adapt the model is retrieved by the algorithms described in Section 4. These methods will retrieve sentences from: (i) the general domain data; (ii) different in-domain datasets; and (iii) from a concatenation of both the general domain and in-domain set. Therefore the research questions we propose to explore are the following three:

1. Can a model fine-tuned with a subset of data outperform the model trained with general domain data?

   The work of Poncelas et al. (2018b) showed that performing fine-tuning on a subset of data (used to build the model) yields small improvements (and not statistically significant at level p=0.01). A limitation in their experiments is that, as BPE is not applied, the vocabulary of the adapted model remains the same as the general model. As in these experiments we are processing the data using BPE, the limitation of the vocabulary should disappear (as sub-words are considered rather than complete words). We are interested in exploring whether performing fine-tuning with a subset of the data (in which BPE was applied) can improve the base model.

2. Can a model fine-tuned with a subset of in-domain data outperform the model fine-tuned with the complete data set?

   The general uses of fine-tuning (Luong and Manning, 2015; Freitag and Al-Onaizan, 2016) consist of using in-domain data set to adapt a model. However, we want to investigate whether applying data selection in smaller *in-domain* set can also lead to improvements.

3. Can a model fine-tuned with a dataset mixture of general-domain and in-domain data outperform the previous-mentioned models?

   By considering both datasets (general and in-domain data), the number of candidate sentences is increased. This also poses a challenge to the transductive algorithm as most of the candidate sentences are not in-domain. We are interested in exploring whether these algorithms can successfully retrieve sentences that lead to improvements.

3 Related Work

There are several adaptation techniques for NMT. Chu and Wang (2018) structure them into two main groups, *data centric* (techniques which involve augmenting or modifying the training data) and *model centric* (techniques which involve modifying the architecture or the procedure with which the model is trained). In this paper, we use a combination of both as we use data selection methods (data centric) and fine-tuning (model centric).

The technique of fine-tuning (Luong and Manning, 2015; Freitag and Al-Onaizan, 2016) consists of training an NMT model with a general domain data set until convergence, and then using an in-domain set for the last epochs.

The work of van der Wees et al. (2017) showed that training an NMT model using less (but more in-domain) data each epoch achieves improvements over a model trained with all data. Their experiments include weighting the sentences using Cross Entropy Difference (Axelrod et al., 2011), and then, each epoch e the top-N_e sentences are used as training data where $N_1 \geq N_e \geq N_{last}$

A proposal in which they use the test set to adapt the model is the work of Li et al. (2018). In particular, they fine-tune a pre-built NMT model for each sentence in the test set. They use three methods to retrieve the sentences that are the most similar to a sentence of the test set: (i) Levenshtein distance (Levenshtein, 1966); (ii) cosine similarity of the average of the word embeddings (Mikolov et al., 2013); and (iii) the cosine similarity between hidden states of the encoder in NMT. The main difference with our work is that they adapt the model sentence-wise (one model for each sentence) whereas the adaptations presented here are document-wise (one model for each test set). Although performing adaptations sentence-wise gives more fine-grained adaptations, it also has several disadvantages: (i) the computational cost is higher as there are several iterations (as many as sentences in the test set) of selecting data and fine-tuning; (ii) the usage of the data is less efficient as a same sentence can be extracted multiple times (in different iterations); and (iii) using different models for each sentence has the potential risk of performing translations that are not consistent throughout the entire document.

4 Transductive Data Selection Algorithms

In this work, we investigate data selection methods that exploit the information of the test set to retrieve sentences. These methods select a subset of from the parallel set (S, T) used as training data. In particular, they select sentences based on overlaps of n-grams between the test set S_{test} and the source side of the parallel data S. In this work, we explore the following three techniques:

TF-IDF Distance Method: Distance methods measure how close two sentences are by using metrics as Levenshtein distance (which computes the minimum number of insertion, deletions or substitutions of characters that are necessary to transform one sentence into the other) to score the similarities. Hildebrand et al. (2005) propose *TF-IDF distance* i.e. to use cosine between TF-IDF (Salton and Yang, 1973) vectors as distance metric. In their work, for each $s_{test} \in S_{test}$ the top sentences from S are selected. Although they are aware that the resulting set contains duplicated sentences, in their experiments the models containing duplicated sentences achieve slightly better results.

TF-IDF measures the importance of the terms in a set of documents. Each document D can be represented as a vector of terms $\mathbf{w}_D = (w_1, w_2, \dots w_{|V|})$, where $|V|$ is the size of the vocabulary. Each w_k is calculated as in (1):

$$w_k = tf_k * log(idf_k) \quad (1)$$

where tf_k is the term frequency (TF) of the k-th term in D, i.e. the number of occurrences, and idf_k is the inverse document (IDF) frequency of the k-th term, as in (2):

$$idf_k = \frac{\#documents}{\#documents\ containing\ term\ k} \quad (2)$$

The similarity between two sentences a and b is computed as the inverse of the cosine distance of their TF-IDF vectors, $\mathbf{w}_a$ and $\mathbf{w}_b$, as in Equation (3):

$$sim(a, b) = 1 - cos(\mathbf{w}_a, \mathbf{w}_b) = 1 - \frac{\mathbf{w}_a \cdot \mathbf{w}_b}{|\mathbf{w}_a||\mathbf{w}_b|} \quad (3)$$

In the TFIDF transductive method, each sentence s in the *Candidate data* S is scored according to the highest similarity with a sentence r from the test set S_{test} computed as in Equation (4):

$$score(s) = \max_{r \in S_{test}} sim(s, r) \quad (4)$$

Infrequent *n*-gram Recovery (INR): Parcheta et al. (2018) propose extracting those sentences containing n-grams from the test set that are considered infrequent (Gascó et al., 2012) (so frequent words such as stop words are ignored).

A sentence s is scored according to the number of infrequent n-grams shared with the set of sentences of the test set S_{test}. It is computed as in Equation (5):

$$score(s) = \sum_{ngr \in \{S_{test} \bigcap s\}} max(0, t - C_L(ngr)) \quad (5)$$

where $C_L(ngr)$ is the count of ngr in the selected set of sentences L (those that have been selected already). t is the number of occurrences of an n-gram to be considered infrequent. If the number of occurrences of ngr is above the threshold t then ngr is considered frequent n-gram (the component $max(0, t - C_S(ngr))$ is 0) and it does not contribute for scoring the sentence. When a sentence is added to the selected pool the count of the n-gram in the candidate data $C_L(ngr)$ is updated (Gascó et al., 2012).

Feature Decay Algorithms (FDA): Feature Decay Algorithms Biçici and Yuret (2011) selects data trying to maximize the variability of n-grams in the selected data by decreasing their value as they are added to a selected pool L, which eventually becomes the selected data.

In order to do that, the n-grams in the test set are extracted and assigned an initial value. Each sentence in the set of candidate sentences has an importance score (i.e. the normalized sum of the score of its n-grams) of being selected.

Then, iteratively, the sentence with the highest score in the candidate data is selected and added to a set of selected pool L. In addition, the values of the n-grams of the selected sentence are decreased to ensure a variability of n-grams. The values are decreased according to the decay function in Equation (6):

$$decay(f) = init(f)\frac{d^{C_L(ngr)}}{(1 + C_L(ngr))^c} \quad (6)$$

where $C_L(ngr)$ is the count of the n-gram ngr in L. c and d are parameters of FDA. By default they have a value of 0 and 0.5, respectively.

The $decay(ngr)$ function in Equation (6) indicates the score of the feature ngr at a particular iteration, so it is dependent on the set of selected sentences L.

The sentence s is scored as a normalized (by length of the sentence) sum of the scores of the features. Considering the default values in Equation (6), the resulting score function is as in Equation (7):

$$score(s, L) = \frac{\sum_{ngr \in F_s} 0.5^{C_L(ngr)}}{\text{\# words in s}} \quad (7)$$

where F_s is the set of n-grams in sentence s.

Once the selected pool L contains the desired amount of sentences, the sentences are retrieved as selected data.

5 Experimental Setup

The data sets used in the experiments are based on the ones used in the work of (Biçici, 2013):

We build German-to-English NMT model using the data provided in the WMT 2015 (Bojar et al., 2015) (4.5M sentence pairs). We consider this data set as the general-domain training data to build the non-adapted NMT (*BASE*). As development data, we use 5K randomly sampled sentences from development sets of previous years.

The BASE model is adapted to two domains: news and health. Therefore we also use two test sets and two *in-domain* training set (for the research question 2 and 3 explained in Section 2):

- News Domain: We use the test set provided in WMT 2015 News Translation Task, and the in-domain *rapid2016*[1] data set (1.3M sentence pairs) provided in WMT 2017 News Translation (Bojar et al., 2017).
- Health Domain: German-to-English parallel text from the European Medicines Agency (EMEA)[2] (Tiedemann, 2009) (361K sentence pairs). For health domain test set we use the Cochrane [3] dataset provided in WMT 2017 biomedical translation shared task (Yepes et al., 2017).

Note that the general-domain set contains sentences from a corpus such as Europarl (Koehn, 2005) which causes the domain to be closer to the news domain.

All data sets are tokenized, truecased and Byte Pair Encoding (BPE) (Sennrich et al., 2016) is applied with 89500 merge operations (the number of operations used in the work of Sennrich et al. (2016)). The models have been built using OpenNMT-py (Klein et al., 2017). We keep the default settings of OpenNMT-py: 2-layer LSTM with 500 hidden units, vocabulary size of 50000 words for each language.

We use different evaluation metrics to evaluate the performance of the models built in the experiments. These models are evaluated on the test sets using several evaluation metrics: BLEU (Papineni et al., 2002), TER (Snover et al., 2006) and METEOR (Banerjee and Lavie, 2005). The scores assigned by this metrics indicate an estimation of the

[1]https://tilde.com/
[2]http://opus.nlpl.eu/EMEA.php
[3]http://www.himl.eu/test-sets

quality of the translation (compared to a human-translated reference). Higher scores of BLEU and METEOR indicate better translation quality. TER is an error metric, therefore lower scores indicate better performance.

In each table, scores that are better than the baseline are shown in bold. Furthermore, scores that constitute a statistically significant improvement at level p=0.01 over the baseline are marked with an asterisk. This was computed with multeval (Clark et al., 2011) using Bootstrap Resampling (Koehn, 2004).

6 Baseline Results

6.1 Baseline Results with General-domain Data

	BASE12	BASE13
BLEU	26.16	26.34
TER	54.41	54.41
METEOR	30.00	30.09

Table 1: Results of the model BASE12 and BASE13 evaluated on the news test set.

	BASE12	BASE13
BLEU	33.29	33.14
TER	46.11	46.79
METEOR	34.62	34.57

Table 2: Results of the model BASE12 and BASE13 evaluated on the health test set.

Table 1 presents the results evaluated with the news test set evaluated in the 12th epoch of the base model (*BASE12*) and the 13th epoch (*BASE13*). Similarly, Table 2 presents the results evaluated with the test set in the health domain. These results help to confirm that the models trained for 12 epochs are close to convergence: In Table 1 the increment in performance from the 12th to the 13th epoch is just of 0.0018 BLEU points and in Table 2 the performance is worse in the 13th epoch.

6.2 Baseline Results With In-domain Data

Following the work of Luong and Manning (2015; Freitag and Al-Onaizan (2016) we adapt the base system (*BASE12*) by performing the 13th iteration in a different, smaller, in-domain data set. We create two new models, one adapted to the domain of

	BASE12	BASE12 + rapid2016
BLEU	26.16	24.05
TER	54.41	55.86
METEOR	30.00	28.74

Table 3: Results of the model BASE12 fine-tuned with the in-domain news set.

	BASE12	BASE12 + EMEA
BLEU	33.29	34.69
TER	46.11	44.43
METEOR	34.62	34.99

Table 4: Results of the model BASE12 fine-tuned with the in-domain health set.

news (*BASE12 + rapid2016*) and another one to the health domain (*BASE12 + EMEA*).

We see, in Table 4, how using in-domain data for fine-tuning can increase the performance with more than 2 BLEU points. However, the data set chosen for performing fine-tuning is important, as in Table 3 we see the performance of the model becomes worse after fine-tuning with the rapid2016 dataset. This also indicates that the addition of new data is not necessarily good.

7 Main Experiments

In order to answer the questions in Section 2, we perform three set of experiments: fine-tune the BASE12 model with a subset of the general domain data (Section 7.1), with a subset of in-domain data (Section 7.2), and with a subset of data retrieved from both general domain data and in-domain data (Section 7.3).

We use the default configuration of the data selection methods. We use $d = 0.5$, $c = 0$ and 3-grams as features in FDA (Equation (6)).

In the INR method we also use 3-grams as ngr (in Equation (5)). In order to find a value of the threshold for the experiments, in this paper we execute several runs of INR using different values of t, multiplying by two in each execution (we try 10, 20, 40, 80 ...). In the experiments we use the highest value of t that fulfills one of the following criteria: (i) the execution time should be under 48 hours or (ii) the number of sentences retrieved at least 500K. Accordingly, the value of t in news domain is 80 (230K sentences retrieved) and in health domain 640 (275K sentences retrieved).

7.1 Results of Models Trained in a Subset of General-Domain Data

	BASE13	BASE12 + TFIDF	BASE12 + INR	BASE12 + FDA
		100K lines		
BLEU	26.34	**26.41**	**26.49**	**26.49**
TER	54.41	54.45	**54.19**	**54.21**
MET.	30.09	**30.14**	**30.21***	**30.21***
		200K lines		
BLEU	26.34	26.33	**26.44**	**26.55***
TER	54.41	54.41	**54.35**	**54.17***
MET.	30.09	30.03	**30.12**	**30.24***
		500K lines		
BLEU	26.34	**26.44**	-	**26.40***
TER	54.41	**54.40**	-	54.47
MET.	30.09	**30.11**	-	**30.10***

Table 5: Performance on the *news* test for the BASE12 model, fine-tuned with subsets of the training data.

	BASE13	BASE12 + TFIDF	BASE12 + INR	BASE12 + FDA
		100K lines		
BLEU	33.14	**33.95***	**33.52***	**33.68***
TER	46.79	**45.99***	**45.92***	**45.97***
MET.	34.57	**34.96***	**34.77**	**34.71**
		200K lines		
BLEU	33.14	**33.97***	**33.88***	**33.96***
TER	46.79	**46.03***	**45.90***	**45.64***
MET.	34.57	**34.89***	**34.94***	**35.01***
		500K lines		
BLEU	33.14	**34.14**	-	**33.75***
TER	46.79	**45.60***	-	**45.92***
MET.	34.57	**34.96***	-	**34.92***

Table 6: Performance on the *health* test for the BASE12 model, fine-tuned with subsets of the training data.

In order to investigate the first question mentioned in Section 2 we select a subset of sentences of the general-domain data (the data set used to build BASE12). We extract subsets of three different sizes: 100K, 200K, and 500K lines. The only exception is the INR method which, with the established configuration, retrieves at most 230K sentences and 275K sentences using the news and health test, respectively. The BASE12 model is fine-tuned for a 13th epoch using the subset of data extracted.

In Table 5 and Table 6 we show the performance of the base model in the first column (*BASE13* column) and then the model in which the last epoch is fine-tuned using data selected by one of the three data selection algorithms. As we can see, fine-tuning the model with the selected data leads to improvements for most of the experiments (numbers in bold).

The vocabulary considered in the fine-tuning is the same used for building the BASE12 model. However, as BPE has been applied, this restriction is less strict. For example, in the sentence of the news test set "das Bildungsministerium teilte mit, etwa ein Dutzend Familien sei noch nicht zurückgekehrt." (according to the reference, "the Education Ministry said about a dozen families still had not returned.") the word "Bildungsministerium" ("Education Ministry") would have been left out (even if in the selected data there are several occurrences) if BPE was not applied because it is infrequent in the general domain set. As in these experiments we use BPE, the adapted models achieves improvements in terms of fluency.

The non-adapted, BASE13 model translates the above-mentioned sentence as "the Ministry of Education said, for example, that a dozen families did not return.". In this sentence, the phrase "for example" has been added. The model adapted using TFIDF (100K lines) generates a similar sentence (i.e. "the Ministry of Education said, for example, that a dozen families had not returned."), but this problem is corrected by the model adapted using INR and FDA (100K lines) as both of them generate the same translation: "the Ministry of Education said, about a dozen families have not returned.". Here the phrase "for example" added by BASE13 model is removed.

7.2 Results of Models Trained with a Subset of In-Domain Data

In order to answer the second research question stated in Section 2, we also execute the same transductive algorithms (using the same configuration) in the in-domain set (i.e. rapid2016 and EMEA). We retrieve the same amount of sentences: 100K, 200K and 500K lines for news domain; and 100K and 200K for the health domain (as EMEA only has 361K sentences).

In Table 7 we show in the first column, *BASE12+rapid2016*, the performance of the model fine-tuned with the complete in-domain

	BASE12 + rapid2016	BASE12 + TFIDF rapid2016	BASE12 + INR rapid2016	BASE12 + FDA rapid2016
		100K lines		
BLEU	24.05	**25.05***	**25.39***	**25.46***
TER	55.86	**55.67**	**55.52***	**55.41***
MET.	28.74	**29.07***	**29.50***	**29.49***
		200K lines		
BLEU	24.05	**24.76***	-	**25.12***
TER	55.86	**55.77**	-	**54.76***
MET.	28.74	**28.91**	-	**29.54***
		500K lines		
BLEU	24.05	**24.59***	-	**24.75***
TER	55.86	**55.67**	-	**55.10***
MET.	28.74	**28.85**	-	**29.33***

Table 7: Performance on the *news* test for the BASE12 model, fine-tuned with subsets of the rapid2016 data set.

	BASE12 + EMEA	BASE12 + TFIDF EMEA	BASE12 + INR EMEA	BASE12 + FDA EMEA
		100K lines		
BLEU	34.69	**35.11**	**35.22**	**35.18**
TER	44.43	45.09	**43.60**	44.94
MET.	34.99	**35.17**	**35.25**	**35.15**
		200K lines		
BLEU	34.69	**35.55**	-	**35.11**
TER	44.43	**44.18**	-	**43.66**
MET.	34.99	**35.70***	-	**35.28**

Table 8: Performance on the *health* test for the BASE12 model, fine-tuned with subsets of the EMEA data set.

rapid2016 set (also presented in Table 3). The other columns contain the evaluation scores after fine-tuning BASE12 model with subsets of rapid2016. Similarly, Table 8 indicates the performance of the model fine-tuned with theEMEA dataset and different subsets (evaluated with health test). Note also that the number of sentences retrieved by INR (using the same configuration as in the previous section) is less than 200K lines, so those experiments are not executed.

Using a subset of in-domain data can improve the performance as again, most of the scores in Table 7 and Table 8 are marked in bold. We see that the impact of the models evaluated in the news domain (Table 7) is higher as all experiments achieve statistically significant improvements at level p=0.01 for at least one evaluation metric. Despite that, none of the models improve the BASE13 model (column BASE13 in Table 1).

7.3 Results of Models Trained with a Mixture of General-Domain and In-Domain Data

As we have seen in previous sections, applying fine-tuning with subsets of data can perform better than using the complete dataset. In this section, we aim to explore the performance of models fine-tuned on data retrieved from a mixture of the two datasets used in previous sections: data used for building the BASE12 model, and in-domain data (rapid2016 or EMEA datasets). These experiments are particularly interesting in the case of news test because using an external dataset led to worse results.

	TFIDF	INR	FDA
	news test		
100K lines	52%	89%	86%
200K lines	50%	88%	87%
500K lines	46%	-	86%
	health test		
100K lines	27%	67%	69%
200K lines	29%	70%	71%
500K lines	31%	-	74%

Table 9: Percentage of base training data lines retrieved.

In Table 9 we present the percentage of lines from the general domain dataset present in the selected data. We observe that in the news domain (the first subtable in Table 9) the percentages are higher than in the health domain (the second subtable). This indicates how these transductive methods are capable of identifying better sentences. As shown in Table 3, the sentences from the base dataset are more useful for the news test as using the rapid2016 set for tuning the model leads to worse results.

If we perform a (column-wise) comparison of the three methods, we can observe that the INR and FDA methods retrieve a similar amount of sentences from the base set. By contrast, the TFIDF method seems to retrieve a smaller amount of sentences from the general domain data (the percentages in column TFIDF of Table 9 are much lower than the other columns).

	BASE13	BASE12 + rapid2016	BASE12 + TFIDF	BASE12 + INR	BASE12 + FDA
			100K lines		
BLEU	26.16	24.05	**26.42**	**26.56**	**26.65***
TER	54.41	55.86	54.57	**53.92***	**54.23**
MET.	30.09	28.74	30.06	**30.21**	**30.25***
			200K lines		
BLEU	26.16	24.05	26.14	**26.40**	**26.59**
TER	54.41	55.86	54.72	**54.25**	**54.22**
MET.	30.09	28.74	29.95	**30.13**	**30.13**
			500K lines		
BLEU	26.16	24.05	**26.24**	-	**26.23**
TER	54.41	55.86	54.53	-	**54.27**
MET.	30.09	28.74	29.99	-	30.02

Table 10: Performance on the *news* test for the BASE12 model, fine-tuned with subsets of a combination of the BASE and rapid2016 data sets.

	BASE13	BASE12 + EMEA	BASE12 + TFIDF	BASE12 + INR	BASE12 + FDA
			100K lines		
BLEU	33.29	34.69	34.48	**34.96**	**34.89**
TER	46.11	44.43	45.28	**44.68**	**44.95**
MET.	34.62	34.99	**35.30**	**35.35**	**35.21**
			200K lines		
BLEU	33.29	34.69	**35.57**	**35.56**	**35.59**
TER	46.11	44.43	**44.23**	44.59	45.54
MET.	34.62	34.99	**35.59**	**35.77***	**35.54**
			500K lines		
BLEU	33.29	34.69	**36.79***	-	**35.78**
TER	46.11	44.43	**43.30***	-	44.88
MET.	34.62	34.99	**36.05***	-	**35.99**

Table 11: Performance on the *health* test for the BASE12 model, fine-tuned with subsets of a combination of the BASE and EMEA data sets.

In Table 10 and Table 11 we show two baselines: (i) column BASE13 shows the model built performing 13 epochs; and (ii) column BASE12+rapid2016 and BASE12+EMEA present the results observed in Table 3 and Table 4, respectively. In those tables we indicate in bold those scores that are better than both baselines.

The models adapted to the news test (Table 10) using INR and FDA tend to perform better than both the BASE13 and the BASE12+rapid2016 models. This is especially true for smaller datasets (the adaptation with 100K lines achieves statistically significant improvements at p=0.01) but becomes closer to BASE13 when more sentences are retrieved (500K lines subtable). For the TFIDF method, despite the fact that it achieves better results than the BASE12+rapid2016 model, most of the scores are worse than the BASE13 model. As mentioned earlier, TFIDF tends to retrieve more sentences from the rapid2016 set (Table 9), and as we saw before using more sentences from this set leads to worse performing models.

In the health domain (Table 11), by contrast, TFIDF performs slightly better (the only experiment that achieves statistically significant improvements at p=0.01 for the three evaluation metrics).

8 Conclusion and Future Work

In this work, we have shown how general domain models can be adapted to a test set by fine-tuning not only to a particular domain but also to a special subset of sentences (retrieved from in-domain or out-of-domain data) that are closer to a test set and achieve better results.

We have seen that fine-tuning a model using a subset of data can achieve better performance than the model trained with the full training set. This is also applicable when using an additional set of in-domain sentences. Nonetheless, the best results are observed when augmenting the candidate sentences (i.e. combining general and in-domain sentences) as presented in Section 7.3.

FDA offers a good balance in performance and speed. INR achieve results similar to FDA, but the execution time is dependent on the configuration (i.e. value of the threshold t) and it may cause to exceed several hours (FDA requires less than one hour for the same execution). The configuration also restricts the amount of sentences retrieved. In the experiments performed, we retrieved no more 200K sentences to evaluate INR whereas for the other TA we could retrieve 500K parallel lines. Moreover, in this work we have used the same values of t for all the experiments, which have been determined following the most restrictive assumption of not knowing the in-domain data. In the future, we want to evaluate the models fine-tuned with data retrieved from INR using different values of t.

TFIDF technique, although achieving comparable results, we find to be the weakest of the TA explored. The main differences with the other two is that is not a context-dependent (i.e. it does not consider the selected pool to retrieve new sentences) and in addition, each sentence is considered independently. This caused that for larger test set such *news*, the improvements tend to be smaller or not to find statistically signifficant improvements at p=0.01 (e.g. tables 5 and 10).

The experiments carried out in this paper can be further expanded using different language pairs, different domains and different selected-data sizes. Moreover, other configurations of data selection algorithms could be investigated. For example, using n-grams of higher order, executing INR with different values of t, in Equation (5), or FDA with different values of d and c, in Equation (6) (Poncelas et al., 2016; Poncelas et al., 2017).

The techniques explored here can also be used in combination with other approaches aiming to adapt models towards a particular domain. The models presented in Section 7.3 can be further expanded by adding a tag in the source sentences indicating the domain explicitly (Chu et al., 2017; Poncelas et al., 2019b), using a target-side seed or using synthetic sentences (Chinea-Rios et al., 2017; Poncelas et al., 2019a).

Acknowledgements

This research has been supported by the ADAPT Centre for Digital Content Technology which is funded under the SFI Research Centres Programme (Grant 13/RC/2106) and is co-funded under the European Regional Development Fund.

This work has also received funding from the European Union's Horizon 2020 research and innovation programme under the Marie Skłodowska-Curie grant agreement No 713567.

References

Axelrod, Amittai, Xiaodong He, and Jianfeng Gao. 2011. Domain adaptation via pseudo in-domain data selection. In *Proceedings of the 2011 Conference on Empirical Methods in Natural Language Processing*, pages 355–362, Edinburgh, Scotland, UK.

Banerjee, Satanjeev and Alon Lavie. 2005. Meteor: An automatic metric for MT evaluation with improved correlation with human judgments. In *Proceedings of the ACL workshop on intrinsic and extrinsic evaluation measures for machine translation and/or summarization*, pages 65–72, Ann Arbor, Michigan.

Biçici, Ergun and Deniz Yuret. 2011. Instance selection for machine translation using feature decay algorithms. In *Proceedings of the Sixth Workshop on Statistical Machine Translation*, pages 272–283, Edinburgh, Scotland.

Biçici, Ergun. 2013. Feature decay algorithms for fast deployment of accurate statistical machine translation systems. In *Proceedings of the Eighth Workshop on Statistical Machine Translation*, pages 78–84, Sofia, Bulgaria, August.

Bojar, Ondřej, Rajen Chatterjee, Christian Federmann, Barry Haddow, Matthias Huck, Chris Hokamp, Philipp Koehn, Varvara Logacheva, Christof Monz, Matteo Negri, Matt Post, Carolina Scarton, Lucia Specia, and Marco Turchi. 2015. Findings of the 2015 Workshop on Statistical Machine Translation. In *Proceedings of the Tenth Workshop on Statistical Machine Translation*, pages 1–46, Lisboa, Portugal.

Bojar, Ondřej, Rajen Chatterjee, Christian Federmann, Yvette Graham, Barry Haddow, Shujian Huang, Matthias Huck, Philipp Koehn, Qun Liu, Varvara Logacheva, et al. 2017. Findings of the 2017 conference on machine translation (wmt17). In *Proceedings of the Second Conference on Machine Translation*, pages 169–214, Copenhagen, Denmark.

Chinea-Rios, Mara, Alvaro Peris, and Francisco Casacuberta. 2017. Adapting neural machine translation with parallel synthetic data. In *Proceedings of the Second Conference on Machine Translation*, pages 138–147, Copenhagen, Denmark.

Chu, Chenhui and Rui Wang. 2018. A survey of domain adaptation for neural machine translation. *arXiv preprint arXiv:1806.00258*.

Chu, Chenhui, Raj Dabre, and Sadao Kurohashi. 2017. An empirical comparison of domain adaptation methods for neural machine translation. In *Proceedings of the 55th Annual Meeting of the Association for Computational Linguistics (Volume 2: Short Papers)*, volume 2, pages 385–391, Vancouver, Canada.

Clark, Jonathan H., Chris Dyer, Alon Lavie, and Noah A. Smith. 2011. Better hypothesis testing for statistical machine translation: Controlling for optimizer instability. In *Proceedings of the 49th Annual*

Meeting of the Association for Computational Linguistics: Human Language Technologies (Volume 2: Short Papers), page 176–181, Portland, Oregon.

Eetemadi, Sauleh, William Lewis, Kristina Toutanova, and Hayder Radha. 2015. Survey of data-selection methods in statistical machine translation. *Machine Translation*, 29(3-4):189–223.

Freitag, Markus and Yaser Al-Onaizan. 2016. Fast domain adaptation for neural machine translation. *arXiv preprint arXiv:1612.06897*.

Gascó, Guillem, Martha-Alicia Rocha, Germán Sanchis-Trilles, Jesús Andrés-Ferrer, and Francisco Casacuberta. 2012. Does more data always yield better translations? In *Proceedings of the 13th Conference of the European Chapter of the Association for Computational Linguistics*, pages 152–161, Avignon, France.

Hildebrand, Almut Silja, Matthias Eck, Stephan Vogel, and Alex Waibel. 2005. Adaptation of the translation model for statistical machine translation based on information retrieval. In *Proceedings of the 10th Annual Conference of the European Association for Machine Translation*, pages 133–142, Budapest, Hungary.

Klein, Guillaume, Yoon Kim, Yuntian Deng, Jean Senellart, and Alexander M. Rush. 2017. Opennmt: Open-source toolkit for neural machine translation. In *Proceedings of the 55th Annual Meeting of the Association for Computational Linguistics-System Demonstrations*, pages 67–72, Vancouver, Canada.

Koehn, Philipp. 2004. Statistical significance tests for machine translation evaluation. In *Proceedings of the 2004 Conference on Empirical Methods in Natural Language Processing*, pages 388–395, Barcelona, Spain.

Koehn, Philipp. 2005. Europarl: A parallel corpus for statistical machine translation. *Machine Translation Summit, 2005*, pages 79–86.

Levenshtein, Vladimir. 1966. Binary codes capable of correcting deletions, insertions and reversals. In *Soviet Physics Doklady*, pages 707–710.

Li, Xiaoqing, Jiajun Zhang, and Chengqing Zong. 2018. One sentence one model for neural machine translation. In *Proceedings of the Eleventh International Conference on Language Resources and Evaluation (LREC 2018)*, pages 910–917, Miyazaki, Japan.

Liu, Lemao, Hailong Cao, Taro Watanabe, Tiejun Zhao, Mo Yu, and Conghui Zhu. 2012. Locally training the log-linear model for smt. In *Proceedings of the 2012 Joint Conference on Empirical Methods in Natural Language Processing and Computational Natural Language Learning*, pages 402–411, Jeju, Korea.

Luong, Minh-Thang and Christopher D Manning. 2015. Stanford neural machine translation systems for spoken language domains. In *Proceedings of the International Workshop on Spoken Language Translation*, pages 76–79, Da Nang, Vietnam.

Mikolov, Tomas, Ilya Sutskever, Kai Chen, Greg S Corrado, and Jeff Dean. 2013. Distributed representations of words and phrases and their compositionality. In *Advances in neural information processing systems*, pages 3111–3119.

Papineni, Kishore, Salim Roukos, Todd Ward, and Wei-Jing Zhu. 2002. Bleu: a method for automatic evaluation of machine translation. In *Proceedings of 40th Annual Meeting of the Association for Computational Linguistics*, pages 311–318, Philadelphia, Pennsylvania, USA, July.

Parcheta, Zuzanna, Germán Sanchis-Trilles, and Francisco Casacuberta. 2018. Data selection for nmt using infrequent n-gram recovery. In *Proceedings of the 21st Annual Conference of the European Association for Machine Translation*, page 219–227, Alacant, Spain.

Poncelas, Alberto, Andy Way, and Antonio Toral. 2016. Extending feature decay algorithms using alignment entropy. In *International Workshop on Future and Emerging Trends in Language Technology*, pages 170–182, Seville, Spain.

Poncelas, Alberto, Gideon Maillette de Buy Wenniger, and Andy Way. 2017. Applying n-gram alignment entropy to improve feature decay algorithms. *The Prague Bulletin of Mathematical Linguistics*, 108(1):245–256.

Poncelas, Alberto, Gideon Maillette de Buy Wenniger, and Andy Way. 2018a. Data selection with feature decay algorithms using an approximated target side. In *15th International Workshop on Spoken Language Translation (IWSLT 2018)*, pages 173–180, Bruges, Belgium.

Poncelas, Alberto, Gideon Maillette de Buy Wenniger, and Andy Way. 2018b. Feature decay algorithms for neural machine translation. In *Proceedings of the 21st Annual Conference of the European Association for Machine Translation*, pages 239–248, Alacant, Spain.

Poncelas, Alberto, Andy Way, and Kepa Sarasola. 2018c. The ADAPT System Description for the IWSLT 2018 Basque to English Translation Task. In *International Workshop on Spoken Language Translation*, pages 72–82, Bruges, Belgium.

Poncelas, Alberto, Gideon Maillette de Buy Wenniger, and Andy Way. 2019a. Adaptation of machine translation models with back-translated data using transductive data selection methods. In *20th International Conference on Computational Linguistics and Intelligent Text Processing*, La Rochelle, France.

Poncelas, Alberto, Kepa Sarasola, Meghan Dowling, Andy Way, Gorka Labaka, and Iñaki Alegria. 2019b. Adapting NMT to caption translation in Wikimedia Commons for low-resource languages. In *35th International Conference of the Spanish Society for Natural Language Processing (SEPLN 2019)*, Bilbao, Spain.

Salton, Gerard and Chung-Shu Yang. 1973. On the specification of term values in automatic indexing. *Journal of documentation*, 29(4):351–372.

Sennrich, Rico, Barry Haddow, and Alexandra Birch. 2016. Neural machine translation of rare words with subword units. In *Proceedings of the 54th Annual Meeting of the Association for Computational Linguistics (Volume 1: Long Papers)*, volume 1, pages 1715–1725, Berlin, Germany.

Silva, Catarina Cruz, Chao-Hong Liu, Alberto Poncelas, and Andy Way. 2018. Extracting in-domain training corpora for neural machine translation using data selection methods. In *Proceedings of the Third Conference on Machine Translation: Research Papers*, pages 224–231, Brussels, Belgium.

Snover, Matthew, Bonnie Dorr, Richard Schwartz, Linnea Micciulla, and John Makhoul. 2006. A study of translation edit rate with targeted human annotation. In *Proceedings of the 7th Conference of the Association for Machine Translation in the Americas*, pages 223–231, Cambridge, Massachusetts, USA.

Tiedemann, Jörg. 2009. News from OPUS - A collection of multilingual parallel corpora with tools and interfaces. In Nicolov, N., K. Bontcheva, G. Angelova, and R. Mitkov, editors, *Recent Advances in Natural Language Processing*, volume V, pages 237–248. John Benjamins, Amsterdam/Philadelphia, Borovets, Bulgaria.

Utiyama, Masao, Hirofumi Yamamoto, and Eiichiro Sumita. 2009. Two methods for stabilizing mert: Nict at iwslt 2009. In *International Workshop on Spoken Language Translation (IWSLT 2009)*, pages 79–82, Tokyo, Japan.

van der Wees, Marlies, Arianna Bisazza, and Christof Monz. 2017. Dynamic data selection for neural machine translation. In *Proceedings of the 2017 Conference on Empirical Methods in Natural Language Processing*, pages 1400–1410, Copenhagen, Denmark.

Vapnik, Vladimir N. 1998. *Statistical Learning Theory*. Wiley-Interscience.

Yepes, Antonio Jimeno, Aurélie Névéol, Mariana Neves, Karin Verspoor, Ondrej Bojar, Arthur Boyer, Cristian Grozea, Barry Haddow, Madeleine Kittner, Yvonne Lichtblau, et al. 2017. Findings of the wmt 2017 biomedical translation shared task. In *Proceedings of the Second Conference on Machine Translation*, pages 234–247.

A Multi-Hop Attention for RNN based Neural Machine Translation

Shohei Iida[†], **Ryuichiro Kimura**[†], **Hongyi Cui**[†], **Po-Hsuan Hung**[†],
Takehito Utsuro[†] **and** **Masaaki Nagata**[‡]
[†]Graduate School of Systems and Information Engineering, University of Tsukuba, Japan
[‡]NTT Communication Science Laboratories, NTT Corporation, Japan

Abstract

Among recent progresses of neural machine translation models, the invention of the Transformer model is one of the most important progresses. It is well-known that the key technologies of the Transformer include multi-head attention mechanism. This paper introduces the multi-head attention mechanism into the traditional RNN-based neural machine translation model. Moreover, inspired by the existing multi-hop architectures such as end-to-end memory networks and convolutional sequence to sequence learning model, this paper proposes an RNN based NMT model with a multi-hop attention mechanism. The proposed multi-hop attention model has two heads, where for each head, a context vector is calculated based on the states of the encoder and the decoder. Then, in the second turn of the context vector calculation, those context vectors are updated depending not only on one's own context vector but also on the context vector of the other head. Experimental results show that the proposed model significantly outperforms the baseline in BLEU score in Japanese-to-English/English-to-Japanese machine translation tasks with and without extended context.

1 Introduction

RNN encoder-decoder model (Bahdanau et al., 2015; Luong et al., 2015; Sutskever et al., 2014) was the state-of-the-art in machine translation. However, it is outperformed by non-recursive encoder-decoder models such as Transformer (Vaswani et al., 2017) and Convolutional Sequence-to-Sequence (Gehring et al., 2017) in recent years. However, RNN is not considered to be inferior to Transformer in all respects. For example, according to Tran et al. (2018), it is reported that Transformer is not good at decoding sentences whose length is not included in the training data and it is weak to long distance dependency. In other words, it is weak against long sentence translation. It seems that Transformer became more powerful than RNN by increasing the number of parameters, but it became weak to long sentences for the same reason.

We propose an RNN based source-to-target attention mechanism where the number of parameters increases by repeating the calculation of multi-head attention for a single-source encoder like multi-hop attention in end-to-end memory networks (Sukhbaatar et al., 2015). In the proposed mechanism, those increased number of parameters are well-tuned so that the overall translation accuracy improves, in particular, for long sentences. The proposed multi-hop attention mechanism is based on the hierarchical attention (Libovický and Helcl, 2017) for multi-source encoders, although, in the hierarchical attention (Libovický and Helcl, 2017), the number of parameters for one input does not increase, unlike in the proposed multi-hop attention mechanism.

In evaluation, we compared the performance of the proposed method with Transformer and RNN encoder-decoder using OpenSubtitles 2018 (Lison et al., 2018) and Asian Scientific Paper Excerpt Corpus (ASPEC) (Nakazawa et al., 2016). To test the power of translating long sentences, we also

Proceedings of The 8th Workshop on Patent and Scientific Literature Translation

Dublin, Aug. 20, 2019 |

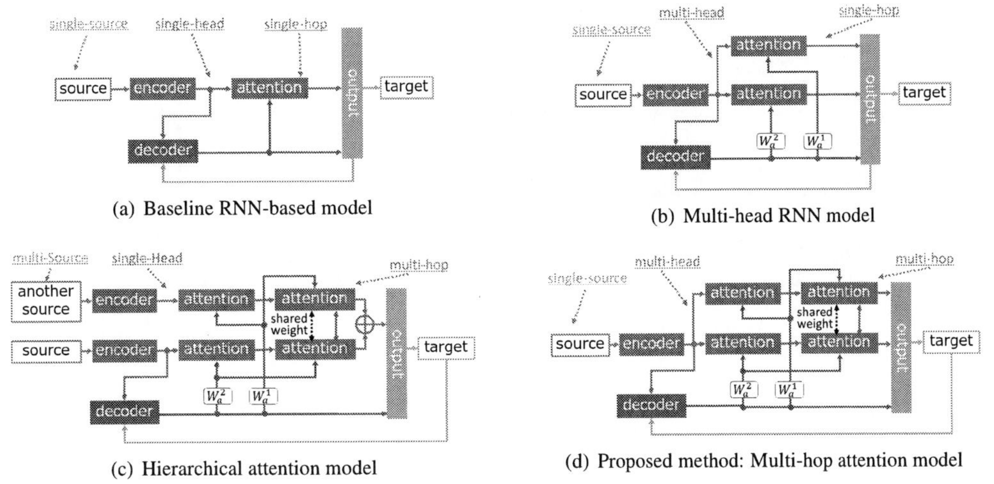

(a) Baseline RNN-based model

(b) Multi-head RNN model

(c) Hierarchical attention model

(d) Proposed method: Multi-hop attention model

Figure 1: Baseline attention and proposed attention

made a context-aware translation model, called 2-to-2 (Bawden et al., 2018; Tiedemann and Scherrer, 2017) for OpenSubtitles 2018. In the Japanese-to-English translation of the ASPEC corpus, the proposed method achieved a significantly better score than the Transformer for long sentences with more than 120 tokens.

In the following sections, we first show previous works on baseline RNN and multi-head RNN encoder-decoders in Section 2. We then describe the proposed multi-hop method in Section 3. We then show the performance for Japanese-to-English and English-to-Japanese translation tasks, focusing on long sentences in Section 4.

2 Neural Machine Translation

2.1 RNN based sequence to sequence NMT

There are two distinctive features in sequence-to-sequence model (Bahdanau et al., 2015; Luong et al., 2015) using RNN (Figure 1(a)). One point is that its encoder and decoder can naturally handle time series and the other point is that it can decide which encoder states in the time series the decoder should pay attention to by introducing a mechanism called source-target attention (Bahdanau et al., 2015; Luong et al., 2015).

In other words, the source-target attention of RNN is designed to deal with time series compared with the self-attention of Transformer where time series are artificially represented using positional embeddings (Vaswani et al., 2017). In this paper, considering this point, we propose a novel model suitable for long sentences by efficiently increasing the number of parameters for source-target attention.

2.2 Multi-head Attention

In this paper, we define multi-head attention with N heads as follows, where $k\ (= 1, \ldots, N)$ denotes the index of the k-th head and $i\ (= 1, \ldots, I)$ denotes the index of the i-th word.

$$s_i^{(k)} = W_a^{(k)} d_i \quad (1)$$

$$c_i^{(k)} = softmax(s_i^{(k)} H^{\mathrm{T}})H \quad (2)$$

In equation (1), the output of RNN decoder d_i is duplicated and converted differently with the weights into multi-head. $W_a^{(k)}$ is a learnable parameter, which duplicated and converted d_i to $s_i^{(k)}$.

In equation (2), dot product attention (Luong et al., 2015; Vaswani et al., 2017) is used to calculate the context vector $c_i^{(k)}$ between k-th head of a decoder state $s_i^{(k)}$ and encoder states H.

When the model has two heads ($N = 2$), the equation (1) and the equation (2) becomes as follows.

$$s_i^{(1)} = W_a^{(1)} d_i \quad (3)$$

$$s_i^{(2)} = W_a^{(2)} d_i \quad (4)$$

$$c_i^{(1)} = softmax(s_i^{(1)} H^{\mathrm{T}})H \quad (5)$$

$$c_i^{(2)} = softmax(s_i^{(2)} H^{\mathrm{T}})H \quad (6)$$

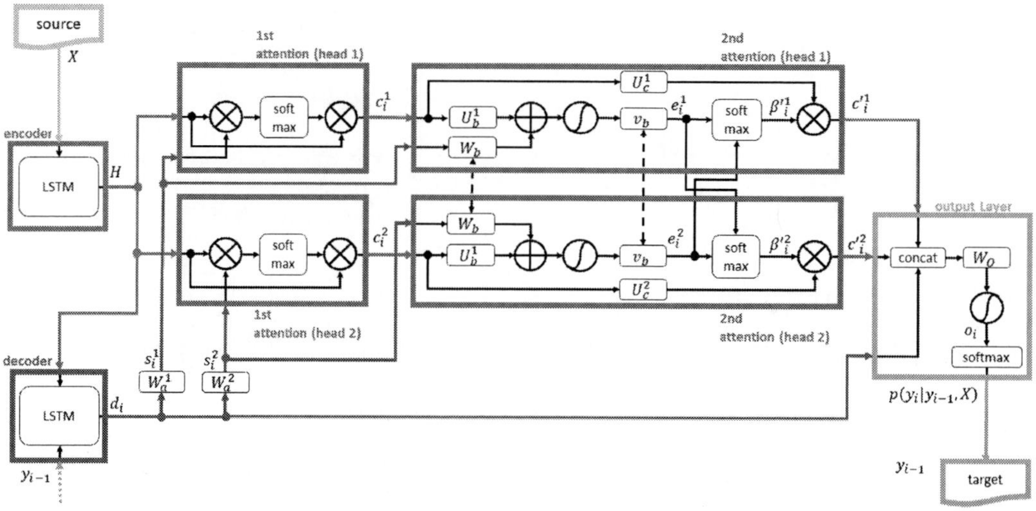

Figure 2: Proposed method detail

As shown in the equation (5) and the equation (6), by using multiple parallel attention via the parameters $W_a^{(k)}$, we expect that each head will attend to a different part of the encoder states.

Chen et al. (2018) attempted to incorporate the various mechanisms of the Transformer into RNN encoder-decoder. They used multi-head attention as shown in Figure 1(b) in source-target attention. Our method becomes the same as their method when we use single-hop attention.

3 Multi-Hop Attention RNN

3.1 Multi-Hop Dependent Attention

To the best of our knowledge, multi-hop attention is first used in end-to-end memory network (Sukhbaatar et al., 2015) to extend the expressive power of RNN. To introduce multi-hop attention into translation, we refer to hierarchical attention (Libovický and Helcl, 2017) in multimodal translation, which combines the context vector obtained from the text and the intermediate expression vector for an image obtained using CNN.

$$e_i^{(k)} = v_b^{\mathrm{T}} tanh(W_b s_i^{(k)} + U_b^{(k)} c_i^{(k)}) \quad (7)$$

$$\beta_i^{(k)} = \frac{exp(e_i^{(k)})}{\sum_{n=1}^{N} exp(e_i^{(n)})} \quad (8)$$

$$c_i'^{(k)} = \beta_i^{(k)} U_c^{(k)} c_i^{(k)} \quad (9)$$

Equation to compute context vector is defined as equation (7), equation (8), and equation (9). Figure 2 is a detailed diagram of the proposed method.

Table 1: Difference between the proposed method and previous studies

Method	source	head	hop
Baseline RNN	single	single	single
Multi-head RNN	single	multi	single
Hierarchical attention	multi	single	multi
Proposed method	single	multi	multi

To illustrate the difference, the proposed method and hierarchical attention are shown in Figure 1(d) and Figure 1(c) and their difference is summarized in Table 1.

In hierarchical attention, since attention is calculated between states of each encoder for multiple source and states of a single decoder, it uses a single-head for each source. On the other hand, our method uses multiple heads for a single source, where attention is directed to different parts of the source sentence and each head influences each other to learn better feature representation. In equation (7), we calculate the attention score between a decoder state $s_i^{(k)}$ and output of the head of the previous hop $c_i^{(k)}$ using Multi Layer Perceptron (MLP) attention (Luong et al., 2015).

The reason for adopting the MLP attention for the second hop instead of the dot product attention used in the first hop (equation (2)) is that the weight of each head can be shared. Since the parameters W_b and v_b in the equation (7) and Figure 2 are shared by all heads, we expect each head can influence each other. According to the report of Vaswani et al. (2017), it is said that dot product attention is superior to MLP attention. However, since it has no parameters to be shared, we assume it is not suitable as an attention mechanism for the second hop.

The equation (8) normalizes the attention score of each head to $\beta_i^{(k)}$ by softmax where n ranges over all heads[1]. Finally, a new context vector $c_i^{\prime(k)}$ is calculated by learnable parameter $U_c^{(k)}$, $\beta_i^{(k)}$, and $c_i^{(k)}$.

When the number of heads N is 2, the above calculation procedure becomes the following:

$$e_i^{(1)} = v_b^{\mathrm{T}} tanh(W_b s_i^{(1)} + U_b^{(1)} c_i^{(1)}) \quad (10)$$

$$e_i^{(2)} = v_b^{\mathrm{T}} tanh(W_b s_i^{(2)} + U_b^{(2)} c_i^{(2)}) \quad (11)$$

$$\beta_i^{(1)} = \frac{exp(e_i^{(1)})}{exp(e_i^{(1)}) + exp(e_i^{(2)})} \quad (12)$$

$$\beta_i^{(2)} = \frac{exp(e_i^{(2)})}{exp(e_i^{(1)}) + exp(e_i^{(2)})} \quad (13)$$

$$c_i^{\prime(1)} = \beta_i^{(1)} U_c^{(1)} c_i^{(1)} \quad (14)$$

$$c_i^{\prime(2)} = \beta_i^{(2)} U_c^{(2)} c_i^{(2)} \quad (15)$$

Finally, we concatenate the N context vectors $c_i^{\prime(k)}$ with the RNN decoder state d_i to obtain the prediction of the output word distribution $p(y_i|y_{i-1}, X)$ where W_o is a learnable parameter.

$$o_i = tanh(W_o[d_i; c_i^{\prime(1)}; ...; c_i^{\prime(k)}]) \quad (16)$$

$$p(y_i|y_{i-1}, X) = softmax(o_i) \quad (17)$$

When the number of heads N is 2, equation (16) becomes the following:

$$o_i = tanh(W_o[d_i; c_i^{\prime(1)}; c_i^{\prime(2)}]) \quad (18)$$

3.2 Multi-Hop Independent Attention

In the multi-hop dependent attention described in the previous subsection, we use the information of other heads and share parameters of MLP attention (W_b and v_b) over all heads (equation (7)) to calculate the secondary context vector $c_i^{\prime(k)}$ (equation (9)).

We also implemented multi-hop independent attention, where the secondary attention is calculated by feed forward neural networks whose parameter is $U_c^{(k)}$ without using MLP attention. In this method, equation (9) is changed as follows.

$$c_i^{\prime(k)} = U_c^{(k)} c_i^{(k)} \quad (19)$$

In this method, since there are no parameters to be shared among heads and no scaling parameters such as $\beta_i^{(k)}$ in equation (8), information of other heads are not used in the secondary attention.

4 Evaluation

In order to confirm the usefulness of the proposed method, this section describes experimental evaluation results in Japanese-to-English/English-to-Japanese machine translation tasks with and without extended context. we used BLEU (Papineni et al., 2002) as the evaluation measure.

4.1 Data

We used the Japanese-English parallel corpora obtained from OpenSubtitles 2018 (Lison et al., 2018) and Asian Scientific Paper Excerpt Corpus (ASPEC) (Nakazawa et al., 2016).

In OpenSubtitles 2018, the total 2,083,576 parallel sentences are divided into 90.0% training data (1,872,077 sentence pairs), 5% development data (102,724 sentence pairs), and 5% test data (108,775 sentence pairs). OpenSubtitles 2018 is a parallel corpus composed of movie subtitles, and their sentences are ordered along the line of the story of the movie. Therefore, in addition to the data used in machine translation tasks without extended context, we created data for context-aware translation according to Tiedemann and Scherre (2017) as follows.

First, given a single pair of a source sentence and a target translated sentence, the source sentence and its immediately preceding sentence are concatenated with a ⟨CONCAT⟩ token, and similarly, the target sentence and its immediately preceding sentence are also concatenated with a ⟨CONCAT⟩ token. By translating the concatenated source sentence pair, a pair of translated target sentences concatenated with a ⟨CONCAT⟩ token is obtained. Then, only the second sentence after the ⟨CONCAT⟩ token is extracted and evaluated. In context translation, this 2-to-2 (Tiedemann and

[1]Haddow et al. (2018) evaluated a similar multi-head and multi-hop attention mechanism, although Haddow et al. (2018) employed the vector concatenation over the multiple heads in stead of normalization. Haddow et al. (2018) also reported that the multi-head and multi-hop attention mechanism outperformed the baseline RNN model in the evaluation of the language pairs of CS-EN, EN-CS, ET-EN, EN-ET, FI-EN, and EN-FI, where the length of the training sentences is limited to 50 words or less. In this paper, on the other hand, in the evaluation of the language pairs of JA-EN and EN-JA, the proposed multi-head and multi-hop attention mechanism outperformed the Transformer when the number of tokens is 120-129.

Table 2: Evaluation Result

Model	head	hop	OpenSubtitles 2018		ASPEC		OpenSubtitles 2018 with context	
			ja→en	en→ja	ja→en	en→ja	ja→en	en→ja
RNN baseline	1	1	12.12	9.27	26.41	36.39	13.85	10.24
Multi-head RNN (single-hop attention)	2	1	12.38‡	9.36†	26.63	36.60†	14.14‡	10.32
	3	1	12.42‡	9.55‡	26.98†	36.55	14.28‡	10.53‡
Proposed Method (multi-hop independent attention)	2	2	12.47‡	9.61‡	26.95†	36.31	14.16‡	10.18
Proposed Method (multi-hop dependent attention)	2	2	12.87‡	9.89‡	27.33‡	36.91‡	14.41‡	10.74‡
	2	3	12.88‡	9.87‡	27.39‡	37.41‡	14.79‡	10.79‡
	3	2	13.03‡	9.83‡	27.27‡	37.54‡	14.83‡	10.55‡
	3	3	13.03‡	9.76‡	27.21‡	37.49‡	14.52‡	10.76‡
Transformer	4	1	<u>15.20</u>	<u>10.95</u>	<u>27.50</u>	<u>38.25</u>	<u>15.98</u>	<u>11.44</u>

Proposed methods that significantly outperform the RNN baseline are indicated by $\dagger(p \leq 0.05)$ and $\ddagger(p \leq 0.01)$.

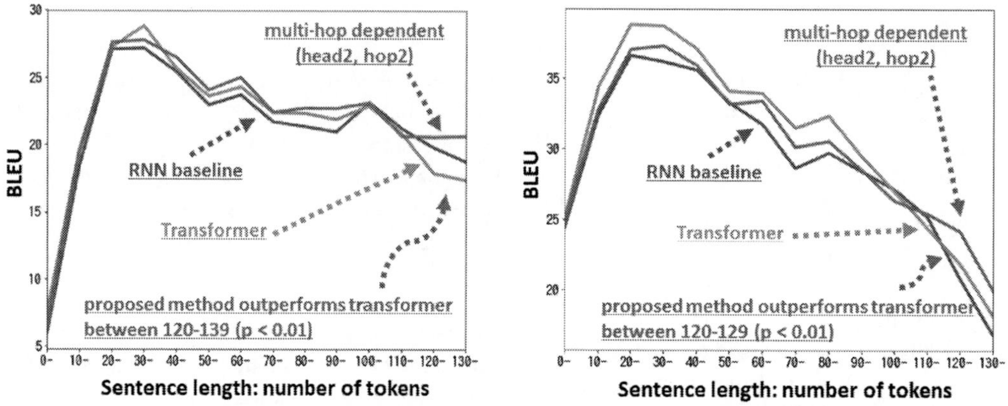

[1]ja→en [2]en→ja

Figure 3: BLEU per sentence length (ASPEC)

Scherrer, 2017) method is a major and increases the number of length per sentence. So, context translation faces long sentence translation.

For ASPEC, among the 3,000,000 training sentence pairs, 1,000,000 sentence pairs with the highest sentence alignment scores were used. Other than the training sentence pairs, 1,790 sentence pairs as the development data as well as 1,812 sentence pairs as the test data are provided by Nakazawa et al. (2016). Also, held out sentence pairs other than those training/development/test data sets are used for the evaluation per sentence length in Section 4.3.

For ASPEC, we conducted an evaluation per sentence length. The widths of the sentence length are segmented with the intervals of 10 words such as 0-9 words, 10-19 words, ..., etc. Each subset for a range of the sentence length is constructed by collecting sentences within that range according to the criterion that the total number of word tokens within each subset is kept as 20,000. Here, for several subsets of short sentences as well as long sentences, held out development sentence pairs with the highest sentence alignment scores are used so as to keep the total number of word tokens within each subset as 20,000. We do not set any upper bound of sentence length in training/development/test. This is for the purpose of evaluating the capability of the proposed method against long sentences.

For tokenization, we used the SentencePiece tool (Kudo and Richardson, 2018) to set the vocabulary size of 32,000 each for both Japanese and English in order to avoid unknown words. Before splitting into subword units by SentencePiece, tokenization is performed by the morphological analysis tool MeCab[2] for Japanese, and by Moses Tokenizer (Koehn et al., 2007) for English[3].

[2]`http://taku910.github.io/mecab/`

[3]By performing tokenization before splitting into subword

Table 3: BLEU per sentence length (ASPEC ja→en)

sentence length	0-9	10-19	20-29	30-39	40-49	50-59	60-69	70-79	80-89	90-99	100-109	110-119	120-129	130-139
number of sentences	1594	1248	810	579	457	372	315	272	238	214	192	176	162	151
RNN baseline	5.94	18.47	27.10	27.16	25.44	22.97	23.71	21.70	21.34	20.96	23.14	21.18	19.78	18.73
multi-hop dependent (head2, hop2)	6.40‡	19.43‡	27.62	27.78	26.49†	24.08‡	25.02‡	22.42	22.74‡	22.72‡	23.11	20.62	20.56††	20.62‡††
Transformer	7.50	19.70	27.29	28.83	25.67	23.62	24.31	22.39	22.34	21.90	22.89	20.80	17.88	17.36

Proposed methods that significantly outperform the RNN Baseline are indicated by †($p \leq 0.05$) and ‡($p \leq 0.01$). Proposed methods that significantly outperform the Transformer are indicated by †($p \leq 0.05$) and ††($p \leq 0.01$).

Table 4: BLEU per sentence length (ASPEC en→ja)

sentence length	0-9	10-19	20-29	30-39	40-49	50-59	60-69	70-79	80-89	90-99	100-109	110-119	120-129	130-139
number of sentences	2531	1303	823	591	458	373	314	272	239	213	193	177	162	108
RNN baseline	24.44	32.41	36.60	36.16	35.58	33.29	31.75	28.65	29.72	28.43	27.14	25.21	20.82	16.86
multi-hop dependent (head2, hop2)	24.90†	32.83	37.03	37.28‡	35.91	33.17	33.40‡	30.12†	30.54	28.52	26.33	25.43	24.18‡††	20.01†
Transformer	25.06	34.41	38.79	38.69	37.09	34.10	33.95	31.49	32.35	29.49	27.00	24.43	21.90	18.22

4.2 Experimental Setup

The baseline is the bidirectional sequence-to-sequence model (Luong et al., 2015) using Long Short-Term Memory (LSTM) which is a kind of RNN. We used fairseq (Gehring et al., 2017) for implementation.

As training, we used Nesterov's Accelerated Gradient (Sutskever et al., 2013) as optimizer with a learning rate of 0.005. The embedding size was 512, the hidden size was 1024, and the encoder and the decoder are of one layer each. For comparison, we also conducted evaluation with the Transformer, where the number of heads was set to 4 according to the default setting[4] of fairseq, and its learning rate was set to 0.0001 following the result of investigating the value at which its loss converged. For all the models, the number of epochs in training was 20. The number of tokens per batch was 2,000 and two GPUs were used in parallel[5].

4.3 Result

Evaluation results are shown in Table 2. Hereafter, as the proposed method without any specific notice, we refer to the model with two heads and two hops of multi-hop dependent attention, which is the model described in Section 3 and Figure 2.

In the evaluation of Japanese-to-English translation of ASPEC, the BLEU of the proposed method was 27.33, which significantly outperforms 26.41 BLEU of RNN baseline. And English-to-Japanese translation of ASPEC, the BLEU of the proposed method was 36.91, which significantly outperforms 36.39 BLEU of RNN baseline. In addition to that, when we measured BLEU for each sentence length, the proposed method significantly outperforms Transformer when the sentence length was between 120 and 129 tokens both direction (Figure 3 [1], Table 3, Figure 3 [2], Table 4). Also, there is no long sentence which has over 120 tokens in the English side of the training corpus.

In multi-hop dependent attention, each head used the information of another head when calculating secondary attention, and two heads shared their parameters. We also evaluated the multi-hop independent attention, where their two heads do not share any information. According to ASPEC's Japanese-to-English translation, the multi-hop dependent attention model achieved the BLEU of 27.33, while the BLEU of the multi-hop independent attention model was 26.95. In the English-to-Japanese translation, the dependent model achieved the BLEU of 36.91, while that of the independent model was 36.31. Both differences are significant at the level of 1% respectively.

In addition, the single-hop attention refers to a model that introduces multi-head attention into source-target attention of RNN and simply increases the number of heads. In the single-hop model with two heads, the BLEU in the evaluation of Japanese-to-English translation of ASPEC was 26.63, which was lower than that of the proposed multi-hop dependent attention model as 27.33. The single-hop attention model is inferior to the proposed multi-hop dependent attention model for all the data sets and both translation directions. Thus, this result supports the usefulness of the proposed multi-hop dependent attention model.

units by SentencePiece, it is guaranteed that any subword unit concatenating over tokenization boundaries is avoided.

[4]Its embedding size is 512, its hidden size is 512, the optimizer used is adam, the encoder and the decoder are of 6 layers each.

[5]The speed of the decoder of the proposed multi-head and multi-hop dependent attention model is roughly two-thirds of that of the baseline RNN model where the numbers of heads and hops are 2.

Table 5: Model Parameters

Model	head	hop	Parameter
RNN baseline	1	1	68,460,544
Multi-head RNN (single-hop attention)	2	1	70,557,696
	3	1	72,654,848
Proposed Method (multi-hop independent attention)	2	2	72,654,848
Proposed Method (multi-hop dependent attention)	2	2	75,800,576
	2	3	81,043,456
	3	2	79,994,880
	3	3	87,334,912
Transformer	4	1	81,604,608

5 Related Works

Dehghani et al. (2019) proposed Universal Transformer for solving the problems of Transformer including the weakness for long distance dependency. Although it has a mechanism to repeat updating the states for each word with parameters shared, it requires a larger number of parameters than Transformer. There could be an approach like BERT (Devlin et al., 2019) where the number of parameters is increased significantly to make a more powerful Transformer model. Our approach, on the other hand, improves the strength of RNN with a little increase of parameters as shown in Table 5. Moreover, Iida et al. (2019) also applied the multi-hop attention mechanism to the Transformer and reported that the Transformer augmented with the multi-hop attention mechanism significantly outperformed the Transformer. Among other existing approaches to neural machine translation, it is known that ConvS2S (Gehring et al., 2017) is equipped with multiple decoder layers where each decoder layer has a separate attention module. The attention of each of those multiple layers is computed and is then fed to another layer, which then takes the fed information into account when computing its own attention etc. The way those multiple attentions are computed is similar to the multi-head and multi-hop attention mechanism proposed in this paper.

6 Conclusion

We proposed a novel multi-hop and multi-head attention mechanism for RNN encoder-decoder in which each head depends on each other repeatedly. We found that the proposed method significantly outperforms the baseline attention-based RNN encoder-decoder. We also found that it outperforms Transformer when the input sentence is very long.

As we showed in Table 2, among the numbers of multi-head and multi-hop, the pair of the numbers of multi-head and multi-hop with the highest BLEU score varies according to the data sets. Considering this fact, one future work is to study how to estimate the pair of the numbers of multi-head and multi-hop with the optimal BLEU score by introducing a held-out development data set.

References

Bahdanau, D., K. Cho, and Y. Bengio. 2015. Neural machine translation by jointly learning to align and translate. In *Proc. 3rd ICLR*, pages 42–51.

Bawden, R., R. Sennrich, A. Birch, and B. Haddow. 2018. Evaluating discourse phenomena in neural machine translation. In *Proc. NAACL-HLT*, pages 1304–1313.

Chen, M. X., O. Firat, A. Bapna, M. Johnson, W. Macherey, G. Foster, L. Jones, M. Schuster, N. Shazeer, N. Parmar, A. Vaswani, J. Uszkoreit, L. Kaiser, Z. Chen, Y. Wu, and M. Hughes. 2018. The best of both worlds: Combining recent advances in neural machine translation. In *Proc. 56th ACL*, pages 76–86.

Dehghani, M., S. Gouws, O. Vinyals, J. Uszkoreit, and Ł. Kaiser. 2019. Universal transformers. In *Proc. 7th ICLR*.

Devlin, J., M.-W. Chang, K. Lee, and K. Toutanova. 2019. BERT: Pre-training of deep bidirectional transformers for language understanding. In *Proc. NAACL-HLT*, pages 4171–4186.

Gehring, J., M. Auli, D. Grangier, D. Yarats, and Y. N. Dauphin. 2017. Convolutional sequence to sequence learning. In *Proc. 34th ICML*, pages 1243–1252.

Haddow, B., N. Bogoychev, D. Emelin, U. Germann, R. Grundkiewicz, K. Heafield, A. V. M. Barone, and R. Sennrich. 2018. The university of Edinburgh's submissions to the WMT18 news translation task. In *Proc. 3rd WMT, Volume 2: Shared Task Papers*, pages 403–413.

Iida, S., R. Kimura, H. Cui, P. Hung, T. Utsuro, and M. Nagata. 2019. Attention over heads: A multi-hop attention for neural machine translation. In *Proc. 57th ACL, Student Research Workshop*.

Koehn, P., H. Hoang, A. Birch, C. Callison-Burch, M. Federico, N. Bertoldi, B. Cowan, W. Shen, C. Moran, R. Zens, C. Dyer, O. Bojar, A. Constantin, and E. Herbst. 2007. Moses: Open source toolkit for statistical machine translation. In *Proc. 45th ACL, Companion Volume*, pages 177–180.

Kudo, T. and J. Richardson. 2018. SentencePiece: A simple and language independent subword tokenizer and detokenizer for neural text processing. *arXiv preprint arXiv:1808.06226*.

Libovický, J. and J. Helcl. 2017. Attention strategies for multi-source sequence-to-sequence learning. In *Proc. 55th ACL*, pages 196–202.

Lison, P., J. Tiedemann, and M. Kouylekov. 2018. Opensubtitles2018: Statistical rescoring of sentence alignments in large, noisy parallel corpora. In *Proc. 11th LREC*, pages 1742–1748.

Luong, T., H. Pham, and C. D. Manning. 2015. Effective approaches to attention-based neural machine translation. In *Proc. EMNLP*, pages 1412–1421.

Nakazawa, T., M. Yaguchi, K. Uchimoto, M. Utiyama, E. Sumita, S. Kurohashi, and H. Isahara. 2016. ASPEC: Asian scientific paper excerpt corpus. In *Proc. 10th LREC*, pages 2204–2208.

Papineni, K., S. Roukos, T. Ward, and W. J. Zhu. 2002. BLEU: a method for automatic evaluation of machine translation. In *Proc. 40th ACL*, pages 311–318.

Sukhbaatar, S., A. Szlam, J. Weston, and R. Fergus. 2015. End-to-end memory networks. In *Proc. 28th NIPS*, pages 2440–2448.

Sutskever, I., J. Martens, George G. Dahl, and G. Hinton. 2013. On the importance of initialization and momentum in deep learning. In *Proc. 30th ICML*, pages 1139–1147.

Sutskever, I., O. Vinyals, and Q. V. Le. 2014. Sequence to sequence learning with neural machine translation. In *Proc. 27th NIPS*, pages 3104–3112.

Tiedemann, J. and Y. Scherrer. 2017. Neural machine translation with extended context. In *Proc. 2017 DiscoMT*, pages 82–92.

Tran, K., A. Bisazza, and C. Monz. 2018. The importance of being recurrent for modeling hierarchical structure. In *Proc. EMNLP*, pages 4731–4736.

Vaswani, A., N. Shazeer, N. Parmar, J. Uszkoreit, L. Jones, A. Gomez, L. Kaiser, and I. Polosukhin. 2017. Attention is all you need. In *Proc. 30th NIPS*, pages 5998–6008.

Decision-making, Risk, and Gist Machine Translation in the Work of Patent Professionals

Mary Nurminen
Tampere University
Kalevantie 4
FI-33100 Tampere, Finland
mary.nurminen@tuni.fi

Abstract

This is the first study on how patent professionals use gist machine translation (MT) in their work. Inductive, qualitative research methods were adopted to explore the role of gist MT specifically in decision-making. Results show that certain decisions by patent professionals rely on gist MT, that the decision to involve human translation is often based on a risk assessment, and that certain factors in the patent environment give affordances for the use of gist MT. The study contributes to the body of knowledge on patent MT users and on gist MT users in general.

1 Introduction

Machine translation (MT) for patents has been developed for a few decades and a broad body of research is devoted to the technologies and techniques for producing patent MT. The professionals who work with patents – patent attorneys, counsels, examiners, etc. – use this MT in its raw, unedited form to obtain a basic understanding, or gist, of patent documents that they need but that are in languages they do not understand. Although their use of this raw MT (termed *gist MT* in this article) has been widespread for approximately a decade, very little research has been conducted on these MT users. In fact, while the number of studies on one group of professionals who use MT in their work, translators, has increased in recent years, research on other professional groups who use the technology remains scarce.

The main objective of this article is to provide the first study focused specifically on the users of patent MT. The article presents the results of a qualitative, exploratory study based on interviews with a small group of patent professionals who use MT in their daily work. Three themes were investigated for the article: the types of decisions patent professionals make based on machine-translated information, the risk assessment they use when deciding between relying on gist MT or opting for human translation, and finally, the environmental factors that appear to give affordances for the use of gist MT in this context.

Two important aspects of patent MT are not in the scope of this study. First, the article does not focus on the issue of quality of MT output, as that has already been studied in numerous other articles. Instead, I wanted to concentrate on exploring other factors that influence gist MT use. Second, another key application of patent MT is its use by professional post-editors to enhance their translation process. These users are not included in the scope of this study.

The article will help to inform research and solution development in the patent MT field. It will also contribute to studies of different professions' use of gist MT and to a general understanding of gist MT users. Better knowledge of how MT is used in different contexts and what contributes to successful use will help us to define what makes a potential use case good, or conversely poor, for gist MT use. In addition, research on experienced users of this form of artificial intelligence can give us insights into the needs of users of other AI technologies.

The structure of the article is as follows: the next section contains a review of related work. This is followed by a description of the data and methods used in this study. Section 4 discusses the types of decisions that patent professionals report making based on gist MT. Section 5 describes the risk assessments that informants appeared to undertake when deciding on ordering human translation. Section 6 focuses on the factors in the work environment that appear to support the use of gist MT. Final conclusions and suggestions for further studies are presented in Section 7.

2 Related work

To the best of my knowledge, thus far no studies have been conducted on how patent professionals use gist MT in their everyday work. A few experimental studies have been done. Larroyed (2018) and Tinsley et al. (2012) describe evaluation experiments in which one evaluation is performed by real patent professionals. A number of studies describe technical solutions for patent MT, and some of those include discussions of some aspects of MT in patent professionals' work, for example, Tinsley (2017), Rossi and Wiggins (2013), and List (2012). In addition to these, a few studies that focus on patent searchers also allude briefly to MT in patent search, including Joho et al. (2010) and McDonald-Maier (2009).

To date there is only a small body of research on professional areas where gist MT is used. Professional translation has been studied to some extent, though in that industry MT is predominantly used for dissemination and not for gisting. Industries with reported use of gist MT include customer support, academia, medicine and the legal field. Customer support groups began to offer multilingual access to knowledge base articles through gist MT in the early 2000s. However, although several articles describe these solutions (e.g. Stewart et al., 2010; Dillinger and Gerber, 2009), very little user experience research has been undertaken, as stated in one of the few studies on actual users (Burgett, 2015: 30). A growing body of research focuses on the use of MT in academia. Much of this focuses on the effects of MT on education and students, but some of the studies also cover educators' viewpoints, such as Bowker and Eghoetz's (2007) study on the acceptability of MT in a university setting and Bowker and Buitrago's (2019) book on using MT in research. Health care is another field where gist MT is beginning to be researched. Liu and Watts (2019) give a good overview of current studies on mobile MT use in health care. Most recently, John Tinsley describes the emergence of new use cases for gist MT in two different industries: legal and life sciences (Beninatto and Stevens, 2019). Both cases are similar to the patent case in that MT is mainly used to sift through large numbers of documents to categorize and then locate the ones that need further scrutiny and possibly human translation.

Work in the area of risk and translation has examined risk assessment and management strategies either as part of the individual translator's work (Pym, 2015; Pym and Matsushita, 2018), or from the perspective of the translation process and service provider (Canfora and Ottmann, 2018). Canfora and Ottmann (2016) present a model for risk management for internal translation processes, including a risk matrix combining the probability of risk and the potential consequences. A recent paper by Nitzke, Hansen-Schirra and Canfora (2019) introduces a model for assessing the risk associated with using post-edited or gist MT. Nonetheless, the focus of that study is primarily the post-editing context, while scenarios involving unedited MT remain mostly unexplored.

3 Methods

The main data for this study was gathered through interviews with nine patent professionals working in Scandinavia. The term *patent professional* in this study refers to professionals in the intellectual property rights (IPR) field who use their expertise in patents to assist and guide others (internal or external groups) in their IPR processes. These professionals hold a variety of titles, such as Patent Counsel, Patent Attorney, and Patent Examiner. The informants for the study are presented in Table 1.

Type of informant	**N**
Patent professionals working in companies that are active in filing and prosecuting patent applications	5
Patent professionals working in an IPR service provider	2
Patent professionals working in a government patent office	2
Total	**9**

Table 1. Informants interviewed for the study

I included informants from the key areas where patent professionals work: private companies, IPR service providers, and governmental organizations. The largest group consisted of professionals working in companies that file patent applications. This is somewhat reflective of the 2010 survey by Joho et al., in which 88% of respondents reported working predominately with internal clients (Joho et al., 2010: 16), which indicates that they worked in patent-filing and prosecuting companies. In addition to the interviews, I gathered background information through talking to people involved in creating and maintaining patent MT solutions.

The average age of the informants was 47 and the average length of experience in the IP field was considerable, 17 years. The group was highly educated; all had at least a master's level education and four of the nine held a PhD degree. This is similar to the educational levels reported in Joho et al. (2010).

The interviews were all semi-structured discussions that occurred either at informants' workplaces or through Skype audio calls. They were conducted in the time frame of April 2018 to February 2019. The two themes of context and transparency were explored in the interviews. I used a variety of sources in the development of the questions. ISO standard 9241-210:2010 (ISO, 2010) defines *context of use* through the broad categories of users, goals and tasks of users, and environment, and this was a good starting point. I relied on descriptions of patent processes in official documents (PRH, 2018; EPO, 2018) and other sources (Alberts et al., 2017; Oesch et al., 2014; Joho et al., 2010) to identify the touchpoints users might have with MT and to develop questions around those touchpoints. The questions also developed somewhat over the course of the data-gathering phase.

Most of the interviews were recorded, transcribed with the aid of automatic transcription tools, and then post-edited. One interview was not recorded due to technical difficulties, so the data from that interview consisted of my notes taken during the interview. A total of 12 hours of interviewing was conducted, and 229 pages of transcription and note data compiled for analysis.

The data was analyzed by closely following the thematic analysis method outlined by Braun and Clarke (2013, 2006, n.d.) with additional guidance from Merriam and Tisdell (2016). The data was approached from a semantic perspective, wherein "coding and theme development reflect the explicit content of the data" (Braun and Clarke, n.d.) rather than searching for underlying meanings in the data. One reason for this was that the topic of the use of technology at work was fairly straightforward. Also, the focus was on the context, as described by informants, instead of each informant's personal experiences.

At a point later in the analysis process, a summary of findings was compiled and a member check performed by three of the informants. They were asked to compare the results against their own experiences and to comment on any incongruences they may detect. These comments were then reviewed and incorporated into the analysis.

A qualitative method was chosen for this study for specific reasons. First, it was necessary because this is the first study on how this group uses gist MT, and research at such an early stage often requires inductive, exploratory methods. When designing the study, there simply was not enough knowledge on these users to allow for the crafting of a quantitative study such as a survey. A second reason was that the small body of research on gist MT users in general tends to rely on surveys and laboratory experiments. I believed there was a need for in-depth studies that would give us a more nuanced view of the use of gist MT. I selected interviewing for data-gathering because it proved difficult to persuade exceedingly busy patent professionals to participate in a study using more time-consuming qualitative methods such as diaries. The interviews required a commitment of only 1.5 hours, which seemed to be more tenable.

4 Decisions that rely on gist MT

Rossi and Wiggins (2013: 116) argue that "In the patent field, MT is used as a support tool for performing novelty, validity, infringement or state-of-the-art searches, and to provide a first understanding of the content of retrieved publications." However, is gaining a "first understanding" really the only way patent professionals use MT, or do they actually make decisions based on gist MT? For example, Henisz-Dostert's study of scientists' use of MT to understand Russian scientific articles reported that, contrary to predictions by early scholars that MT would be used only for scanning, scientists used MT "more as a tool of information than as a tool for the selection of information." (Henisz-Dostert, 1979: 180). One goal of this study was to explore the ways in which patent professionals use gist MT and the decisions they make with its help.

4.1 Relevance

One of the primary uses for patent MT, as defined by Tinsley (2017: 411) is "[to] provide an on-demand 'gist' translation of foreign patents for information purposes to determine relevance." The primacy of using gist MT for this purpose was also found in this study. Informants described how they used gist MT when searching for 'prior art' (patent documents that show that an invention is not new and therefore present an obstacle to patenting it). For each patent document (either a patent or a patent application) found in their search, they need to decide whether it is relevant to the IPR process they are working on or not. Informants discussed four main IPR processes in which they use machine-translated information to determine relevance: (1) the patenting process (Does this invention show enough novelty that it could be patented?), (2) freedom to operate (Can we launch our products in this market or are there patents that we would be infringing on if we launched?), (3) monitoring (Is this patent application sufficiently relevant to our work that I should monitor its progress?), and (4) infringement (Is this patent infringing on one of our patents or are we in danger of infringing on someone else's patent?).

The results of this study reveal that the decision on relevance is very often made without the help of human translation. Therefore, the first decision made is not whether or not a patent document should be sent for human translation, but whether or not it appears to be relevant, and that is determined largely on the basis of gist MT:

> *I would say it's* [the use of MT] *successful in 90 percent of the time because the conclusion is, this is not relevant...So rejecting things from further analysis I think is done 9 out of 10 reviews of the machine translated documents.* (PP4) [1]

It is important to note that the decision on relevance is not as minor a decision as it may seem. The consequences of mistakenly discarding a patent document that seems irrelevant can be considerable, as was reported by informants:

> *...for example I can decide about a patent that it is not in any way relevant for us, which is a pretty strong decision, because then we shut it out completely, the whole followup of the patent, and we just think that that won't be harmful, but then it could be that if there's a mistake in the translation then it turns out that it really **is** harmful. But those are the kinds of decisions I make.* (PP1) [2]

> *At work we talk about how most mistakes take place because someone **overlooks** a relevant patent...when a mistake happens, it is most likely to be caused by that. But mistakes can come from other reasons than the machine translation. There are just so many patents to go through. But putting it into the 'not interesting' pile is a risk.* (PP3)

4.2 Monitoring

A second type of decision that is very often made based solely on gist MT is the decision to tag a patent application for monitoring. If an application is deemed relevant, patent professionals may decide to follow its progress throughout its prosecution. Besides being used to determine enough relevance for monitoring, Gist MT is also used to understand communications on the application's prosecution or to review changes in the application. Tagging an application for monitoring also often means that the decision on human translation is postponed, because the application will most likely change before it is granted:

> *...if it's about pending patents then the claim scope is changing all the time, so therefore even if you would translate it and get it kind of right in the beginning, it's something different when it's granted...so therefore there's no point maybe to get it human translated at the early stage* (PP2)

4.3 Patenting and opposition

A third area in which informants reported using gist MT in decision-making was during the patenting process. Within the European context, the role of MT in the examination process is explained in official guidelines:

> *In order to overcome the language barrier constituted by a document in an unfamiliar non-official language, it might be appropriate for the examiner to rely on a machine translation of said document...A translation has to serve the purpose of rendering the meaning of the text in a familiar language...Therefore mere grammatical or syntactical errors which have no impact on the possibility of understanding the content do not hinder its qualification as a translation.* (EPO, 2018, Part G, Chap. IV-4)

Patent examiners typically share the results of their patentability search with patent applicants, and any relevant patent document that is in another language is provided in machine-translated form. Unless the applicant decides it is so important that they will provide a human

[1] Here and elsewhere: PP = Patent Professional. Also, quotes have been edited for fluency.

[2] Some quotes and passages translated by author.

translation, prosecution proceeds based on the machine translation. MT is occasionally used in opposition proceedings as well:

> PP9: *I mean normally in opposition cases at the EPO, European Patent Office, you can use machine translations.*
> Interviewer: *OK. And in the Finnish patent office as well?*
> PP9: *Yes you can do that. I have never been asked to provide a human translation about any of these.*

5 Deciding on human translation: an exercise in risk assessment

As far as translation is concerned, the most important decision patent professionals or patent applicants make is whether to rely on gist MT for understanding a relevant document or to have it translated by a human. Nitzke et al. (2019) proposes that this type of decision involves risk and that an assessment of those risks should be part of the process of decision-making. Evidence of such a risk assessment emerged in this study, with patent professionals weighing various factors before deciding on gist MT or human translation. The factors that supported human translation of a patent document included the riskiness of the IPR process in which the document would be used, the assumed relevance and importance of the other-language document, and the potential consequences if a misunderstanding would occur due to an error in the gist MT. The factors supporting the use of gist MT were lower costs, quicker access to information, and trust that the patent document is adequately understood. This assessment was summarized by some informants:

> *...the more important decision, the less you do the decision based only on the machine translation.* (PP8)

> *...if the context is clear then it's OK as I see it, I trust the machine translations enough, but sometimes when we are in borderline decisions it's required to have a proper human translation...So it's more a question of the uncertainty margin of the translation with respect to what we are deciding.* (PP4)

Each side of this assessment is examined more closely below.

5.1 Arguments for human translation

One of the top considerations for triggering human translation was the IPR process the other-language relevant document would be used in, with some processes being seen as more high-risk than others. Cases that involved infringement or freedom to operate might involve considerable costs and legal involvement, and these were consequently cited as cases in which human translation is often needed:

> *It depends on the costs involved in the case...if you are in a patent battle, if there is an infringement case...there's a lot of money involved. If you want to be absolutely sure then you have to have a human translator.* (PP9)

If, based on the gist MT, a patent document appears to be highly relevant and important to a case, that would also serve as a strong argument for triggering human translation:

> *...probably that also depends a little bit on the case. If it is highly important then I would choose immediately to get it translated, or claims or parts of it, translated with human translation.* (PP2)

Informants also mentioned potential consequences as a factor in the decision on human translation:

> *If we make the wrong decision and allow a product to the market which does not have freedom to operate, there is a risk of using time and money and goodwill in a court case and potentially being responsible to cover the damages of a client.* (PP4)

5.2 Arguments for relying on gist MT

The main arguments for using gist MT are clearly that translation is very quick and does not generate extra costs. MT is provided at no cost by various national and international patent offices such as the Japan Patent Office and the EPO, and it is commonly included by default in commercial patent search tools. Its use is also made easy through tight integration to patent search tools and processes.

A complete understanding of the arguments for relying on MT in the risk assessment, however, requires consideration of another important element: how strong is the patent professional's trust that they have a sufficient understanding of a patent document? Much of this depends on the quality of the machine translation, of course. However, past studies have shown that other factors can enhance users' abilities to understand MT, and those were reported as helpful in this study as well. Two factors appeared to contribute to trust in understanding in this case study: the fact that patent professionals rely on other resources than the gist

MT, and the background knowledge that patent professionals possess. These are discussed further in the following subsections.

Understanding does not depend on MT alone

The understanding of the machine translation of a patent document can be seen as a process of trying different alternatives until a sufficient level of understanding is achieved. The first alternative is to combine the gist MT with other resources, such as drawings and chemical formulas in the original-language patent documents, to enhance understanding. This combining of MT and auxiliary, often multimodal, information to obtain an understanding of other-language texts has been reported in other studies on MT users (Nitzke et al., 2019; Pituxcoosuvarn et al., 2018; Suzuki and Hishiyama, 2016; Way, 2013; Gaspari, 2004; Henisz-Dostert, 1979). Auxiliary information had a clear role in patent professionals' reports of their work in this study as well:

> *When it's good enough that I can see that it's relevant? It's a combination of understanding the figures and understanding the machine translated text.* (PP6)

> *Oh yeah then you have to look at the original because it doesn't translate any of those chemical formulas...And then if they are totally different then it could be that I don't even make any translation because then I know that, well, they are talking about totally different things.* (PP7)

A second alternative patent professionals resort to are alternative machine translations from other MT tools, a practice that has been noted in earlier studies (Gao et al., 2015; Tinsley et al., 2012). At least one commercial patent search tool offers users access to both their own MT solution and the alternative of Google Translate in the same window. Although a few informants mentioned using a general tool such as Google Translate for alternative translations, a more common method was to try the MT tools provided by specific governmental patent offices:

> *I do the EPO machine translation first and if that's not more understandable then I go directly to the patent office that the publication came from, so Chinese or Japanese.* (PP5)

> *...for instance if it's a Chinese document I go to Chinese Patent Office website and try to find the same application there...and usually it's a different machine translation and that actually helps sometimes, when you have two machine translations you can read them at the same time and maybe it gives you a better impression.* (PP6)

The next alternative professionals can turn to are the other patent professionals they collaborate with. Instead of ordering a human translation of a text that is not sufficiently understood, they can ask the patent professionals who work more closely with the inventors (for example, the patent professionals in the country which the patent originates from) to clarify unclear passages for them.

Background knowledge aids understanding

As mentioned previously, the informants of this study were both highly experienced in the IPR field and well educated. Their contextual knowledge and competences in languages appeared to be important factors in helping them understand and use machine-translated information effectively.

The importance of MT users' knowledge of context in helping them understand machine-translated texts has been reported in a number of studies. Henisz-Dostert (1979) found that a user's familiarity with the subject matter was seen as the main factor in determining the understandability of machine-translated texts. Other studies that have highlighted the importance of contextual knowledge include Bowker and Buitrago (2019), Yasouka and Björn (2011), Yamashita et al. (2009) and Smith (2003).

In the patent context, contextual knowledge is often divided between the patent professionals, who know the patent genre, and the inventors or researchers behind the patents, who know the subject matter better. These competences, their role in helping to understand machine-translated patents, and the division of expertise between patent professionals and inventors were a common theme in the interviews.

> *And when you understand...if we're talking about patent publications there's a certain structure and there's a certain format that they're in, then it's in a way easy easier to follow.* (PP2)

Several previous studies have examined the role of users' language competence in gist MT scenarios (Nurminen and Papula, 2018; Nurminen, 2016; Henisz-Dostert, 1979). In the current study, this background competence also appeared to be a factor in successful use of MT. Although none of the informants spoke English as their native language, all used English daily in their work. Their MT use was mainly from other languages into English, not into their native languages. Besides English, all informants had varying levels of competence in other languages, with German being the most often mentioned, followed by French, Spanish, Swedish, Italian, Dutch, and Japanese. Several informants indicated that competence in the source language helped them to understand texts that were machine-translated from those languages:

> *And quite often I actually combine a machine translation and original reading...the complementarity of understanding the structure of the language better than the machine, and the machine understanding more words than I do, is a good complementarity.* (PP4)

However, the reality is that the major languages patent documents are translated from are Chinese, Japanese, and Korean because these countries are significant producers of patents. China became the world's largest patent producer in 2011. By 2017, China had filed 1.3 million patent applications, more than double the number filed by the second country, the U.S. (WIPO, 2018: 40). The predominance of China was mentioned in all interviews. We can assume from this that competence in the three major patent languages of Chinese, Japanese, and Korean would be particularly useful for patent professionals.

6 Affordances in the patent context

Thus far this article has presented a scenario in which patent professionals can and do use gist MT to make certain decisions. The article has also discussed the factors involved in their decisions to rely on gist MT or to order human translation. However, in the analysis of this study's data, certain contextual factors emerged which appeared to make affordances for the use of gist MT. These affordances must be considered when discussing this specific case because they appear to play an important role in making the use of gist MT tenable, and an understanding of this ecosystem's use of gist MT is incomplete without them. The following sections explore two factors of affordance, risk tolerance and legitimacy.

6.1 Risk-tolerant environment

In the book titled *Translation Quality Assessment*, Andy Way states that MT systems need to be evaluated with the knowledge of what the system would be used for. Way also notes that "[o]f course, some objectives could be more tolerant of MT errors than others" (Way, 2018: 170). Certain features of the patent environment, while perhaps not fully error-tolerant, appeared to make affordances for the risks and potential errors tied to the use of gist MT.

The patenting process is long and iterative, with multiple parties often reviewing the same or similar texts. Different stakeholders may have different interpretations of a patent application's scope and claims. To address these issues, the process contains space for discussion and mechanisms for stakeholders to examine and challenge each other's work. One of these is explained in the Finnish Patent and Registration's Patent Guide:

> *Even though inventions must show absolute novelty, it is not possible for patent authorities to clarify all public information when examining an application. For this reason, the examination process is augmented by the third-party observation and opposition processes, in which third parties, for example competitors, can bring to the attention of the authorities issues that did not emerge during the examination of the patent application. (PRH, 2018: 19)*

The nature of this process means that there are also multiple stages where errors in the understanding of gist MT can be detected and corrected. This was described by one informant:

> *Well of course you can get the wrong impression of the subject matter in the document, but I don't see that it's a really big risk because the patent application process is a long process, so if my interpretation of some kind of document based on the machine translation is wrong, I can change my mind later, if I see it. It takes usually over two years to get a patent so we get the answer from the applicant and we probably write another office action and then the applicant replies again, so it's a conversation. So during the process there's many times when these things can be dealt with.* (PP6)

Another informant described a case when parties examined and challenged each other's MT work:

> *We've had these cases where the examiner used Google Translate and we translate it using EPO's official site and then we can explain to them that 'now we would like to kindly point out that the translation used by the examiner contained a mistake in this spot, and that we have this in that same spot, and our version uses the terms in this way.' And we rely on the [machine] translation completely...the examiner doesn't understand Japanese and we don't understand Japanese. We are both relying on machine translation and there is nothing else.* (PP1)

Besides the risk tolerance present in processes, the informants in this study displayed a tendency to accept the risk involved with using MT and making decisions based on it. One reason for this might be that the informants were vastly experienced. Another reason might be that the IPR field contains other risks besides the use of gist MT, so the organizations they work in might have a higher willingness to take risks, or "risk appetite" as defined by Nitzke et al. (2019). Finally, the acceptance of risk might be an acknowledgement that the risk is simply necessary due to the impossibility of relying on human translation for the large volumes of documentation they regularly encounter, as voiced by one informant:

> *Yes, there is always risk involved. But we have so many patents to go through. Hundreds and hundreds at a time. It would be impossible if all of those had to be translated by a human. Always a risk though.* (PP3)

6.2 Legitimacy of MT

One aspect of the use of MT in the patent environment that I did not expect when I began my research was the legitimacy that it enjoys. One of Merriam-Webster's definitions for *legitimate* best reflects what it means in this context: "conforming to *recognized* principles or *accepted* [emphasis by author] rules and standards."[3] Three different themes in this study illustrated this legitimacy: MT use was transparent, the boundaries of its legitimacy were documented and generally agreed upon by users, and its users had a relatively high level of 'MT literacy.'

Transparency

Transparency in gist MT use has been addressed in a few reports, most recently in a 2019 Globally Speaking Radio podcast in which John Tinsley reported that the legal profession is beginning to use MT for e-discovery, and that its use is fully transparent in that context: "So you go into the court and say to the judge, 'We are taking this position on the basis of a machine translation of this document into English,' and that's legally defensible" (Beninatto and Stevens, 2019).

At least in the European context of this study, the first sign of transparency was the inclusion of MT in EPO guidelines. Second, descriptions by study informants depicted an environment in which the role of MT is transparent to all. They also reported that MT is transparent to secondary users of patent MT, the internal and external clients the patent professionals work with. The results of searches these clients receive from patent professionals often include documents that are machine-translated. These are clearly marked as machine translations and they often also include the date and MT tool that produced the text. Patent professionals discuss MT with the secondary users, as in this example:

> *I would point out that this is a machine translation and, depending on if the client is a knowing patent engineer, then I would maybe give my opinion if we need a proper translation or not, but then ask what they think.* (PP8)

Boundaries of legitimacy

An important aspect of legitimacy is that it is bound to a specific scope. The 'recognized principles or accepted rules and standards' referred to in the definition provided earlier are agreed upon by a certain group for a certain purpose, and the boundaries of applicability are recognized by the participants. In this study, the boundaries of legitimacy for MT were sometimes mentioned during answers to other questions: "For information purposes, it's fine. For use as a legal text, no." (PP3) But in the interviews I also asked directly, "In what situations is it not OK to use machine translation?" The responses indicated some agreement on the areas in which MT should not be used, such as when filing patent applications:

> *...when you're translating your application to other languages – like we have seen some kind of, I think they are usually applicants from Asia, that file an application here and usually they apply in English, but you can really see that their application is machine translated from the Chinese version – not OK.* (PP6)

There was very clear agreement that MT should not be used in legal settings, as in this example in which an informant described a process involving another company's potential infringement of their patent:

> *We would start with searching prior art and use MT. Our aim is to see if there's overlap with our patent or not. If we find something that looks in-*

[3] https://www.merriam-webster.com/dictionary/legitimate

teresting, then we would order human translation of it. We would not just go ahead on that with machine translated information. (PP3)

MT literacy

In 1993 Church and Hovy defined six "desiderata" for a good use case for MT. Among the six were: "it should set reasonable expectations" and "it should be clear to the users what the system can and cannot do" (Church and Hovy 1993: 257). Bowker and Buitrago (2019) expanded this idea by coining the term *MT literacy,* and then applying it to the case of MT use in academic work. On the basis of their definition, I described MT literacy for the context of this study as a patent professional's ability to: (1) comprehend the basics of how machine translation systems process texts, (2) understand how machine translation systems are or can be used (by oneself or others working with patents) to find and read patent documents within the context of IPR processes, and (3) appreciate the wider implications associated with the use of machine translation. Based on this definition, the informants in this study displayed a generally high level of MT literacy. They appeared to understand the basics of MT technologies, knew how to access different MT tools, and were aware of the possibility and consequences of translation errors. They also had experience with different types of MT tools and noticed improvements in quality over time:

> *They all* [languages] *have become better, and especially nowadays if you make a machine translation for some 'normal' language, for German or French, they are really good.* (PP9)

Perhaps one of the clearest signs of the high level of general MT literacy was an observation I made throughout the study: the hype issues currently visible in other spheres (for one example, see Hassan et al., 2017 followed by Toral et al., 2018) do not seem to be occurring in patent MT. In the present study, MT was considered to be one tool among others and people were aware of its uses and limitations. I heard no reports of overreaching claims on MT capabilities.

7 Conclusions

The main objective of this study was to explore the types of decisions patent professionals make based on machine-translated information, the risk assessment they use when deciding between relying on gist MT or using human translation, and the environmental factors that appear to support the use of gist MT in this context. The results revealed that patent professionals routinely make decisions on relevance and monitoring based on gist MT, and that the patenting process also relies on it. In the key decision of initiating human translation, patent professionals tend to weigh the riskiness of the IPR process in which the translated patent document would be used, the assumed relevance and importance of the document, and the potential consequences of misunderstanding against the lower costs, quicker access to information, and trust in a good enough understanding of the patent document. That understanding is often based not only the gist MT, but also other factors, such as auxiliary information sources and patent professionals' contextual and linguistic knowledge. The environmental factors of risk tolerance and legitimacy for gist MT also support the use of MT.

The study contributes to our knowledge of how people, and specifically professional groups, use gist MT. It explores factors that can enhance the use of gist MT, and this understanding will help us to define the characteristics of good, as well as poor, contexts for gist MT use. In addition, this analysis contributes to the growing body of research on users of various types of artificial intelligence.

This study had certain limitations. The group of informants was small and somewhat homogeneous, and this influenced the results. Data was gathered through only one method, interviewing. The results also focused on patent work in one geographical area and one specific point in time, and the results cannot be considered representative of the larger population of patent professionals. Nevertheless, as the first exploratory study of this very experienced group of MT users, it fulfilled one of the main purposes of inductive research in that it uncovered new themes and hypotheses on how a specific group uses gist MT and on the contextual factors that contribute to their use of it.

Further studies on this gist MT user group could target an expanded group of informants, including more diverse participants, other patent MT user groups, and less experienced patent MT users. Studies incorporating other methods such as contextual inquiry, diaries, or quantitative methods such as surveys could verify some of the findings of this study and might reveal further insights on this user group. In addition, it is hoped that we will see a growth in the research, and number of researchers, devoted to studying all types of users of gist MT.

References

Alberts, Doreen, Cynthia B. Yang, Ken Koubek, Suzanne Robins, Matthew Rodgers, Edlyn Simmons, and Dominic DeMarco. 2017. Introduction to Patent Searching. In Lupu, Mihai, Katja Mayer, Noriko Kando and Anthony J. Trippe, editors, *Current Challenges in Patent Information Retrieval*, Second ed. Vol. 29, Springer, Berlin Heidelberg.

Beninatto, Renato and Michael Stevens. 2019. What's the Latest with Neural MT? *Globally Speaking Radio* (podcast), episode 75. RWS Moravia.

Bowker, Lynne and Jairo Buitrago Ciro. 2019. *Machine Translation and Global Research: Towards Improved Machine Translation Literacy in the Scholarly Community,* Emerald Publishing, Bingley, UK.

Bowker, Lynne and Melissa Ehgoetz. 2007. Exploring User Acceptance of Machine Translation Output: A Recipient Evaluation. In Kenny, Dorothy and Kyongjoo Ryou, editors, *Across Boundaries: International Perspectives on Translation Studies*, Cambridge Scholars Publishing, Newcastle, UK.

Braun, Virginia and Victoria Clarke. 2013. *Successful Qualitative Research: A Practical Guide for Beginners.* SAGE, Los Angeles, California, USA.

———n.d. Thematic analysis: reflexive approach, accessed March-June, 2019. https://www.psych.auckland.ac.nz/en/about/our-research/research-groups/thematic-analysis.html

———2006. Using thematic analysis in psychology. *Qualitative Research in Psychology,* 3(2):77–101.

Burgett, Will. 2015. Unmoderated Remote Usability Testing of Machine Translation Content. *TAUS Review of Language Business and Technology,* IV:30–37.

Canfora, Carmen and Angelika Ottmann. 2018. Of ostriches, pyramids, and Swiss cheese: Risks in safety-critical translations. *Translation Spaces,* 7(2):167–201.

———2016. Who's afraid of translation risks? Presentation at 8th EST Congress, Aarhus, Denmark.

Church, Kenneth W. and Eduard H. Hovy. 1993. Good Applications for Crummy Machine Translation. *Machine Translation,* 8:239–258.

Dillinger, Mike and Laurie Gerber. 2009. Success with Machine Translation: Automating Knowledge-Base Translation, Part 1. *ClientSide News*, 10.

EPO: European Patent Office. 2018. Guidelines for Examination in the European Patent Office. European Patent Office, Munich, Germany.

Gao, Ge, Bin Xu, David Hau, Zheng Yao, Dan Cosley, and Susan R. Fussell. 2015. Two is Better than One: Improving Multilingual Collaboration by Giving Two Machine Translation Outputs. *18th ACM Conference on Computer Supported Cooperative Work & Social Computing,* Vancouver, BC, Canada, 852–863.

Gaspari, Federico. 2004. Online MT Services and Real Users' Needs: An Empirical Usability Evaluation. *6th Confererence of the Association for Machine Translation in the Americas, AMTA 2014,* Washington DC, USA 74–85.

Hassan, Hany, Anthony Aue, Chang Chen, Vishal Chowdhary, Jonathan Clark, Christian Federmann, Xuedong Huang, Marcin Junczys-Dowmunt, Will Lewis, Mu Li, Shujie Liu, Tie-Yan Liu, Renqian Luo, Arul Menezes, Tao Qin, Frank Seide, Xu Tan, Fei Tian, Lijun Wu, Shuangzhi Wu, Yingce Xia, Dongdong Zhang, Zhirui Zhang, and Ming Zhou. 2018. Achieving Human Parity on Automatic Chinese to English News Translation. https://arxiv.org/abs/1803.05567

Henisz-Dostert, Bozena. 1979. Users' evaluation of machine translation. In Winter, Werner, editor, *Machine Translation*. Mouton Publishers, The Hague.

ISO. 2010. Ergonomics of Human-System Interaction. Part 210, Human-Centred Design for Interactive Systems (ISO 9241-210:2010*)*. Suomen standardisoimisliitto SFS, Helsinki, Finland.

Joho, Hideo, Leif Azzopardi, and Wim Vandervauwheded. 2010. A Survey of Patent Users: An Analysis of Tasks, Behavior, Search Functionality and System Requirements. *3rd Information Interaction in Context Symposium*, New Brunswick, NJ, USA 13–24.

Larroyed, Aline A. 2018. Machine Translation and Disclosure of Patent Information. *IIC - International Review of Intellectual Property and Competition Law,* 49(7):763–786.

List, Jane. 2012. Review of machine translation in patents - Implications for search. *World Patent Information,* 34(3):193–195.

Liu, Nancy Xiuzhi and Matthew Watts. 2019. Mobile Translation Experience: Current State and Future Directions. In Xu, Xiaoge, editor, *Impacts of Mobile use and Experience on Contemporary Society,* IGI Global, Hershey, PA, USA.

McDonald-Maier, Lisa. 2009. esp@cenet: Survey reveals new information about users. *World Patent Information,* 31(2):142–143.

Merriam, Sharan B. and Elizabeth J. Tisdell. 2016. *Qualitative Research: A Guide to Design and Implementation*. John Wiley & Sons, San Francisco, CA, USA.

Nitzke, Jean, Silvia Hansen-Schirra, and Carmen Canfora. 2019. Risk management and post-editing competence. *The Journal of Specialised Translation,* (31):239–259.

Nurminen, Mary. 2016. Machine Translation-Mediated Interviewing in Qualitative Research: a Pilot Project. *New Horizons in Translation Research and Education*, 4:66–84.

Nurminen, Mary and Niko Papula. 2018. Gist MT Users: A Snapshot of the Use and Users of One Online MT Tool. *21st Annual Conference of the European Association for Machine Translation*, Alicante, Spain 199–208.

Oesch, Rainer, Heli Pihlajamaa, and Sami Sunila. 2014. *Patenttioikeus* [Patent Law]. 3rd ed. Talentum, Helsinki, Finland.

Pituxcoosuuvarn, Mondheera, Toru Ishida, Naomi Yamashita, Toshiyuki Takasaki, and Yumiko Mori. 2018. Machine Translation Usage in a Children's Workshop. *10th International Conference on Collaboration Technologies,* Costa de Caparica, Portugal, 57–73.

PRH: Patentti- ja rekisterihallitus [Finnish Patent and Registration Office]. 2018. *Patenttiopas* [Patent Guide].Patentti- ja rekisterihallitus, Helsinki, Finland.

Pym, Anthony. 2015. Translating as risk management. *Journal of Pragmatics,* 85(Aug):67–80.

Pym, Anthony and Kayo Matsushita. 2018. Risk Mitigation in Translator Decisions. *Across Languages and Cultures,* 19(1):1–18.

Rossi, Laura and Dion Wiggins. 2013. Applicability and application of machine translation quality metrics in the patent field. *World Patent Information,* 35(2):115–125.

Smith, Ross. 2003. Overview of PwC/Sytranet on-line MT Facility. *Twenty-Fifth International Conference on Translating and the Computer*, London, UK.

Stewart, Osamuyimen, David Lubensky, Scott Macdonald, and Julie Marcotte. 2010. Using Machine Translation for the Localization of Electronic Support Content: Evaluating End-User Satisfaction. *The 9th Conference of the Association for Machine Translation in the Americas,* Denver, Colorado, USA.

Suzuki, Hiroshi and Reiko Hishiyama. 2016. An Analysis of Expert Knowledge Transmission using Machine Translation Services. *Seventh Symposium on Information and Communication Technology*, 352–359.

Tinsley, John. 2017. Machine Translation and the Challenge of Patents. In Lupu, Mihai, Katja Mayer, Noriko Kando and Anthony J. Trippe, editors, *Current Challenges in Patent Information Retrieval*, Second ed. Vol. 29, Springer, Berlin Heidelberg.

Tinsley, John, Alexandru Ceausu, Jian Zhang, Heidi Depraetere, and Joeri Van de Walle. 2012. IP-Translator: Facilitating Patent Search with Machine Translation. *AMTA-2012: Tenth Biennial Conference of the Association for Machine Translation in the Americas*, San Diego, CA, USA.

Toral, Antonio, Sheila Castilho, Ke Hu, and Andy Way. 2018. Attaining the Unattainable? Reassessing Claims of Human Parity in Neural Machine Translation. *Third Conference on Machine Translation*, Brussels, Belgium 113–123.

Way, Andy. 2018. Quality Expectations of Machine Translation. In Moorkens, Joss, Sheila Castilho, Federico Gaspari & Stephen Doherty, editors, *Translation Quality Assessment: From Principles to Practice*, Springer, Cham, Switzerland.

Way, Andy. 2013. Traditional and Emerging use-Cases for Machine Translation. *Translating and the Computer,* London, UK.

WIPO: World Intellectual Property Organization. 2018. World Intellectual Property Indicators 2018. World Intellectual Property Organization, Geneva, Switzerland.

Yamashita, Naomi, Rieko Inaba, Hideaki Kuzuoka, and Toru Ishida. 2009. Difficulties in Establishing Common Ground in Multiparty Groups using Machine Translation. *CHI 2009, the SIGCHI Conference on Human Factors in Computing Systems*, Boston, MA, USA 679–688.

Yasouka, Mika and Pernille Bjorn. 2011. Machine Translation Effects on Communication: What Makes it Difficult to Communicate through Machine Translation? *IEEE*, Kyoto, Japan 110-115.

Author Index

Association for Computational Linguistics
209 N. Eighth Street
Stroudsburg, Pennsylvania 18360

ISBN 978-1-5108-9250-7

CURRAN ASSOCIATES INC.
proceedings.com